WIELDING
THE
SWORD

WIELDING THE SWORD

Preachers and Teachers
of God's Word

Linda Finlayson

CF4·K

Published by
Christian Focus Publications,
Geanies House, Fearn, Tain, Ross-shire,
IV20 1TW, Scotland, Great Britain.
Tel: +44 (0)1862 871011
Fax: +44 (0)1862 871699
www.christianfocus.com
e-mail: info@christianfocus.com

Cover design by Daniel van Straaten
Cover illustration by Fred Apps
Inside Illustrations by Fred Apps
Printed and bound by Nørhaven, Denmark.

For Donna Farley,

my lifelong friend, fellow writer

and Eastern sister in Christ.

Contents

Thank You

I would like to thank a number of people for their help in writing this book. Even though the author's name appears on the front cover, many people worked behind the scenes to make this book possible.

I wish to thank all those who helped with my research: answering my many questions, recommending books to read and reading my manuscript to hunt for errors. They are: James R. Ginther, Carl R. Trueman, Lawrence R. Farley, Donna Farley, Sharon L. Bratcher, Marsha Blake, Grace Mullen, Karla Grafton, Spencer W. Ewing, and Sandy Finlayson, my husband. If there are any mistakes left in this book, they are entirely the author's responsibility. I would also like to thank Catherine Mackenzie and Christian Focus for encouraging me in my writing and for their willingness to publish my books.

Setting the Prisoners Free
Padua, Italy 1231

Anthony rose from his prayers as the bell rang for Prime. His knees creaked as he stretched his sore body after the long hours he had spent kneeling. In the pre-dawn dark, he made a slight effort to straighten his rough friar's habit and felt with his feet for his worn leather sandals. Finding them at the foot of his narrow bed, he slipped them on and went to join his fellow friars as they filed past his cell to the chapel. At this time of the morning the only other sounds Anthony usually heard were a few songbirds greeting the day while the city of Padua began to wake. Oddly, today he could hear a steady murmuring and shuffling of feet coming from the streets. Who could be making that noise at this time of day?

After their simple prayer service the friars gathered in the refectory to prepare for the day. No food would be served this morning. It was Lenten season and the friars were fasting. A light meal of bread and beer would be served later in the day. By this time the sun was streaming in the windows and the noise from the streets below had risen to a noticeable level. Friar Angelo went to the window to investigate.

After leaning far out, Angelo pulled his head back inside and exclaimed, 'Friar Anthony, look! I've never seen so many people all in one place before. And they are still coming in the city gates, from all around the countryside. Isn't it wonderful?'

Anthony frowned as he went to join his fellow friar at the window. Angelo was right. The narrow street was full of people and so was the piazza at the end. Not one square inch of cobble-stoned street could be seen. Anthony shook his head.

Angelo laughed. 'O come now, Brother. Be glad! All these people have come to hear you preach. And not just the poor people. Rich people and merchants. Shopkeepers have shut up their shops. Even the city leaders, and the priests and bishop. All to hear you!'

'Then I won't preach,' Anthony replied, sitting down abruptly on a wooden bench, his olive-skinned face set in determination.

Brother Angelo sobered and put his hands on his hips. 'What do you mean you won't preach? God has given you the gift of speaking and the gift of learning to understand His Word. Why would you refuse to use those gifts?'

Anthony shook his head again, sighing heavily. 'Brother Angelo, if these people have only come to have their ears tickled with fancy words or well-spoken arguments then they should all go home. They should only come to hear God speak, not me. God gives his gifts to be used for his glory, not mine.'

'Of course,' Angelo agreed. 'But how will they hear God's Word except someone preach to them? These people are hungry to hear what you can tell them about God. Otherwise, they would have stayed in their homes and their shops. Go to them, Brother, and feed them.'

Anthony suddenly felt sorry for his hasty answer to Angelo's enthusiasm. 'You are right and I am wrong. Thank you, Brother, for your kind words of rebuke.'

When the wooden doors to the friary were pushed opened, Anthony was amazed at the sea of people.

'How will we get to the church?' he asked aloud.

'I don't think you can preach in the church today, Brother,' Angelo replied. 'Not even a fraction of these people will get to hear you. I think we need to have you stand on the hillside outside the city. Then everyone can gather round to hear you.'

'But how will we get there?' Anthony wanted to know.

'We'll take care of that,' replied Friar John, as he stepped in front of Anthony. John, the tallest of the friars, then directed the rest to form a circle around Anthony and walk as a group while John broke open a path for them through the crowds.

'Make way! Make way for Friar Anthony!' John called out in a loud voice.

Most of the people parted respectfully, but some tried to press closer to the now-famous preacher. Anthony walked with his head bowed, shrinking away from any who tried to touch him. He was very troubled that all these people thought that he was special.

Once they passed through the city gates and across the bridge over the River Brenta, the group of friars led Anthony up to the top of a hill, scattering a few sheep that were munching on the spring grass. Behind them the crowd surged through the gates and formed a huge semi-circle at the bottom of the hill. A couple of men laden with tools and some boards pushed their way through and began to climb up the gentle slope with their burdens. One of them hastily explained that they could build a small platform for Friar Anthony. Once that was accomplished Anthony climbed up on the platform and looked out over the crowd.

Friar Angelo was right. People dressed in the richest clothing to those wearing the poorest rags stood below him; thousands of them now silent, waiting for him to speak. Anthony had been preaching every morning since Lent had begun the month before. At first only small crowds had gathered in the church. Then the crowds had grown to fill the town piazza. Now they had come from all the surrounding towns and filled the valley below. *Please let me say the right words,* Anthony prayed silently, and then he opened his mouth to preach.

'Do you think you can continue to live each day without a thought for God?' Anthony challenged his audience. 'Do you think that God cannot see what you do, what you say and even what you think? Do you not fear coming face to face with the great Creator, the mighty God, to answer for your sins?'

No one moved. No one spoke or even whispered. They all stared straight up at the friar who was looking down at them. Anthony had lived in Padua for over four years and knew the people well. He knew that some of the more important families were constantly feuding, trying to cheat each other in business dealings and threatening to harm each other. He knew there was a group of women who lived sinful lives and weren't even ashamed of it. He knew that some of the city officials took bribes regularly and some of the bankers charged such high interest rates that they had driven many to poverty. He knew there were thieves in the audience and people who regularly lied in the courts for money. And he knew the poor were despised and ill-treated. Anthony knew that these people needed God's message of judgment and hope.

So Anthony told them how their sinful behaviour looked to a holy God who is perfect, warning them of God's anger at sin. And then he told them of God's love and how Jesus, God's Son, had come to die for their sins.

'That was a dark day when Jesus died, loaded down with all your sins and mine. How he suffered! And not for his sin, for he was sinless! He did it for you and for me. Then God turned that darkness into light when he raised his Son from the grave. Death was defeated and hope is now offered to all who will receive it.'

The crowd began to stir. Some were weeping at the description of Jesus' death and resurrection. But Anthony didn't stop there.

'You must repent of your sin. You must confess all that you have done wrong to your heavenly Father so you may have forgiveness. You who constantly fight with others must confess your anger. You who are greedy must confess that you have made an idol of your wealth. You who lie and scheme must humble yourself before God and ask for his forgiveness.'

Now many people were weeping and some had fallen to their knees with their heads bowed. But Anthony still wasn't finished.

'Repentance and confession are the first steps. But it is not enough to ask for and receive God's great gift of forgiveness. Your whole life must change. You can no longer sin against your loving Heavenly Father or against your brother or neighbour. Your lives must show that you belong to God. You must turn from your wicked ways and obey God's commandments.'

By the time Anthony had finished speaking, most of the people were full of remorse for the way they had been living. So Anthony encouraged those who wanted to confess their sins to come forward and he and other priests from the surrounding churches met with them. For the rest of that day Anthony sat and listened and prayed with each of the people who knelt down before him. And after each confession he advised them to show their remorse by making restitution for their sin. A thief had to return either the item he had stolen or the money to pay for it. Those who were feuding must make up their quarrels and promise to help one another. Those who had oppressed the poor by charging high interest rates must lower their rates and share their profits with the poor. And so it went on until the sun began to set and Anthony was feeling faint with hunger.

At last he and the rest of the priests and the friars were free to return to the city. As they entered the friary, Anthony saw Podesta Stefano Badoari pacing impatiently in the courtyard, his fur-lined woollen cloak flying out behind him with every turn. As a city official, he was used to having people wait for him, not the other way around. But when he saw Anthony his scowl changed to a smile and he came forward to greet the famous preacher.

'Friar,' Stefano said as he bowed to Anthony. 'I've been waiting a long time to speak with you.'

'I had to care for the people,' Anthony replied. 'What did you want?'

Stefano looked at the group of curious friars. 'I'd like to make a confession,' he said with some embarrassment.

Anthony almost scolded him for not lining up with the crowds earlier, but instead motioned for the Podesta to follow him to the chapel. After Anthony was seated, Stefano hitched up his long tunic to kneel down and began to confess his sins. Once he finished he rose quickly and turned to leave.

'Wait,' said Anthony, not entirely convinced that the Podesta was serious about what he had just done. 'What changes will you make in your life now?'

'Changes?' Stefano asked. The important man was genuinely puzzled.

Anthony frowned and then stood up. 'Come with me,' he said and he led the way back out of the chapel and the friary. Together the friar and the city leader walked down the stone streets to the city prison.

'What are we doing here?' Stefano asked nervously. 'Surely you don't want to go in there!'

That was exactly what Anthony wanted to do and he called to the guard to bring a torch. With the flaming length of wood held high Anthony walked through the iron gate that the guard held open and motioned to Stefano to follow. Gathering his fine woollen cloak around him, the man stepped carefully through the entrance.

Almost immediately Stefano let go of his cloak and raised his arm to cover his nose. The nasty, dank odours of the dirty dungeon together with all those people who had not bathed for a long time made him feel ill. As they walked through the prison, Anthony held the torch so they could look into the cells. Peering over his sleeve, Stefano could see that each cell was crowded, some with whole families in them: young children, parents and grandparents. The people shied away from the brightness, not used to light and ashamed to be seen. And it was cold. Everyone huddled together trying to stay warm with the few blankets they had been given.

Anthony stopped and turned to the city magistrate. 'Look!' he commanded.

Stefano bristled. 'But they broke the law,' he replied defensively. 'They belong there.'

'This is a debtors' prison,' Anthony stated and Stefano nodded. 'These people were charged exorbitant interest rates when they fell on hard times. When they couldn't pay their debts the bankers had them arrested and brought here.'

'Of course,' Stefano agreed. 'That's the law. If you can't pay your debts you go to prison until the debt is paid.'

'And how do they pay the debt when they are in prison?' Anthony asked, his anger rising.

Stefano shrugged. 'It's the law.'

'And who makes the laws in Padua?' Anthony demanded impatiently.

Stefano's eyes widened. 'You want me to change the law? But what about their debts? If they were foolish enough to borrow money they shouldn't have, or spend more than they made, why shouldn't they be in prison?'

'Because it's unjust! They're not criminals, only poor people. Our Lord commanded us to care for the poor, not imprison them!'

Anthony led the troubled Podesta out of the prison, handing the torch back to the waiting guard. Turning to Stefano, Anthony explained his idea. 'Podesta, you have been given the power to make just laws. Instead of sending people to prison for debts, why not have them turn over whatever they have to the bankers in payment. That way the debt is paid and people are free to begin again.'

Stefano thought for a moment. 'It's never been done that way before, but I think that's a good idea. I will have the new law drawn up tomorrow. Thank you, Friar. I think I see now what you mean by our lives changing.'

'Good,' Anthony replied. 'God has shown you compassion by forgiving your sins. Now you go and show that same compassion to the people of this city.'

The following week the new law was passed and read out to the people of Padua.

In the Name of the Father and of the Son and of the Holy Spirit. Amen. At the request of the venerable Friar (and holy confessor) Anthony of the Order of Friars Minor it was established and ordained that henceforth no one is to be held in prison for any pecuniary debt or debts, whether past, present or future, if he shall have agreed to relinquish his possessions; and that is to be understood both of debtors and of their guarantors. Furthermore, if any renunciation or cession or alienation shall have been fraudulently made by the debtors or the guarantors, this renunciation or cession shall not be valid nor have legal effect nor work to the prejudice of the creditors. And if such fraud cannot be proved to have taken place, the case shall rest with the judgment of the Podesta.

That day the prison doors were opened and all those who had been imprisoned for debt were released. Most of them came to the friary to thank Anthony for his part in making the new law. He refused their praise and instead directed them to God.

'You have been given a second chance.' Anthony told them. 'Use it wisely. Honour God, repent of your sins and live lives that bring glory to him.'

* * *

Anthony died later that year, much to the sorrow of the city of Padua. But they had listened carefully to his teaching and preaching and the city became a more peaceful, well-ordered place to live.

Anthony was only one of the many men and women that God has used through the centuries to teach and preach for him. Let's read about some others in the Bible that God called to carry out this special task of speaking God's words.

Bubbling Fountains:
Biblical Prophets and Teachers

Way back in Bible times, God chose men and women to speak his words for him so that his people would know two things: what God wanted them to do and what God promised to do for them. These chosen people were called prophets. The word prophet today has come to mean someone who predicts future events. Back then the word meant much more than that. Since the Old Testament was written in the Hebrew language, the first word used to describe a prophet was the Hebrew word *nabi*. *Nabi* means bubbling forth, like a fountain of water. That gives us a picture of words pouring out of a person's mouth like water bubbles out of a fountain. And not only that, but a fountain is lovely to listen to, almost like music.

Other Hebrew words were also used to explain what a prophet did. The words *ro'eh* and *hozeh* both mean 'seer' or one who tells what is going to happen. But we must be very clear here. God's prophets were not magicians, predicting the future to entertain people. God gave them messages to preach that sometimes included what God had planned for their futures. Later, when the Bible was translated into Greek and Latin, another word was chosen with a plainer meaning: *prophetes* meaning speaker. If we put together all those words we have a picture of a speaker who is lovely to listen to as he bubbles or pours forth God's words. Those were the kind of people that God wanted speaking for him.

Now you might think if that was the case then all of God's chosen prophets would have nice messages from God. Some did, but God also had difficult things for them to say: terrible warnings and judgments. And that's where the voice of the speaker mattered too. They had to speak out with confidence and conviction, knowing that they were speaking the truth and saying it in God's name. So let's have a look at some of the people that God chose for this important job. Notice, too, that God chose different kinds of people, each one the right person for the task God had in mind.

Samuel (Eleventh century B.C.)

Samuel grew up in the tabernacle after his mother Hannah had dedicated him to the Lord God. So Samuel knew from early on in his life that he was going to be serving God as a priest. He lived with Eli, the priest, and his family and Eli trained him to carry out all the duties of a priest. What Samuel didn't know, until one special night, was that God had more than just priestly work for him to do.

Samuel was around twelve years old, and had been living and working in the tabernacle for about eight years. That night was just like any other night. He had finished his work and put out the lamps except the Lamp of God, which was left burning all night in the tabernacle. Then he settled down to sleep not far from where Eli was already sleeping. Sometime in the night Samuel heard his name being called. That wasn't such a surprise. Eli was getting to be an old man and couldn't see very well, so he sometimes called for Samuel to help him. Samuel replied, 'Here I am,' and went to see what his teacher needed. But Eli told him he hadn't called him so Samuel went back to bed. However, just as he got comfortable, he heard his name called again. Samuel, being obedient, got up again and went to Eli and said, 'Here I am, for you called me.' Again Eli said, 'I didn't call you, my son; lie down again.' Samuel must have been really confused. Why had this happened twice? If Eli wasn't calling him, who was? When it happened the third time, Eli realised that God was calling Samuel. Eli told Samuel, 'Go, lie down, and if he calls you, you shall say, "Speak, Lord, for your servant hears"'.

Samuel must have been wide awake by now and maybe a little afraid. It was rare for someone to hear God speak to them and

Samuel wasn't even a grown man. He must have wondered why God had chosen to speak to him. When he did hear his name called, just like the other times, Samuel answered as Eli had instructed him. And then God told Samuel some awful news. God was going to punish Eli's family. Eli's grown sons had disobeyed God and had refused to listen to their father when he told them to stop. Samuel must have been very sorry to hear such a judgment on the man who was like a father to him. But the next morning when Eli asked what God had said, Samuel reluctantly told him the bad news. Eli's response was a good example to Samuel. Eli bowed his head and accepted what God had said without complaint. And just as God had said, the judgment came a short time later.

That night was the beginning of Samuel's job as a prophet. From that time onward, God gave Samuel many things to say to the people of Israel, some comforting and full of promises, some fearful things full of judgment. But everyone knew that Samuel spoke the true words of God and knew that they should listen and obey.

Elisha (*c.* 850-795 B.C.)

Elisha was the son of a wealthy farmer and his family lived in Israel during the prophet Elijah's lifetime. Now it's important not to get the names of these two men confused even though their names look similar. Elijah was older than Elisha and already a well-known prophet in Israel. He was the one who had challenged the prophets of the false god Baal to a contest on Mount Carmel and won with the dramatic help of the living God.[1] Not long after that exciting event, Elijah arrived at Elisha's father's farm during spring ploughing. Elisha must have been startled. What was the man of God doing here? Then Elisha was even more surprised when Elijah took off his cloak and threw it around Elisha's shoulders. Elisha knew at once that this was very important. Elijah wasn't just being kind because he thought that Elisha was cold. Elijah, the prophet,

---

[1] You can read about the contest in 1 Kings 18.

was making the announcement to everyone that Elisha had been chosen by God to be a prophet.

Elijah then left with his cloak and continued walking on his way. Elisha ran after him. When he caught up to the older man, Elisha asked Elijah for permission to go and say goodbye to his parents. Elijah agreed but reminded him not to find excuses to stay longer than necessary. God himself had called Elisha to leave farming and be his spokesman. Elisha made his farewells and offered a sacrifice to God before he left his family behind to follow Elijah.

Elisha's training began that day. He spent all his time with Elijah and other prophets in Israel. Even though Israel was ruled by evil kings like Ahab and Ahaziah, there were still those who loved God and served him. Elisha must have been a good student because he soon became known as the one who would take Elijah's place after he died. So when God told Elijah that his time was near, Elijah took Elisha with him on a farewell tour of the cities and towns where the other prophets lived: Gilgal, Bethel and Jericho. When they stopped at each city Elijah said to Elisha, 'Stay here.' But Elisha refused. He knew that his beloved teacher was about to die and he wanted to spend every minute with him. Finally, they came to the Jordan River where Elijah performed a miracle by rolling up his cloak and hitting the water with it. The river parted for them to cross without getting wet. After they reached the other side Elijah, the old prophet, said to his student Elisha, 'What can I do for you before I'm taken?'

Elisha answered right away, asking for a double portion of God's spirit so that he could do the work of a prophet well. Elijah replied that he had asked for a difficult thing, but if Elisha would stay with him to the end what he asked for would be given to him. Elisha, the loyal student, stayed and watched as God took his teacher into heaven in a fiery chariot. That must have been an amazing moment: the excitement of seeing such a miraculous event, the terrible sadness that his teacher was gone, and the knowledge that he, Elisha, was now to take his teacher's place. Elijah's cloak had fallen to the ground when he was taken up to heaven, so Elisha took off his own outer clothing and wrapped himself in the prophet's cloak. It was now his turn to wear it.

We are not told what it was like for Elisha to receive the double portion of God's spirit that he asked for, but when he returned to the prophets living in Jericho they knew without being told. They showed him respect by bowing down before him.

Elisha lived a long life and performed miracles as well as delivering God's messages to the people and the kings. During his lifetime he saw four kings of Israel. Three did evil in God's sight, but the last one served God. There were wars and economic difficulties, people who threatened his life and those who sought his help. Throughout his life, Elisha remained true to God by preaching God's Word.

Peter (*c.* 1 B.C. – A.D. 67)

Peter was a fisherman, although his name wasn't Peter when he was growing up in Bethsaida on the shore of the Sea of Galilee. His parents had named him Simon. Simon joined his father's fishing business, along with his brother Andrew, after he had finished his schooling at the synagogue. He also worked with his neighbours, James and John and their father Zebedee. Being a fisherman meant long hours of work, especially during the early hours of the day and sometimes through the night. But that didn't mean that Simon and Andrew weren't interested in serving God too. Andrew went to hear John the Baptist preach, and through John the Baptist, met Jesus for the first time. Then Andrew invited his brother to come with him to meet the Messiah too. Simon did and the first thing Jesus said was, 'So you are Simon the son of John? You shall be called Peter.'[2]

That must have been a surprise for Simon, now Peter, until you look at what the two names mean. 'Simon' means listener, and 'Peter' means rock. Simon Peter was a rough and tumble sort of person who spoke his mind and sometimes regretted it later. Jesus

---

[2] John 1:42

was giving Simon Peter a hint of what was to come. Peter was going to need to be as strong as a rock if he was going to follow Jesus. But he still had to be a listener, too, because Peter had much to learn.

A short time after their first meeting, Jesus, God's son, came to the shore where Peter and Andrew were washing their nets after a long night of fishing. With Jesus came a large crowd eager to hear him preach. So Jesus asked Peter for a loan of his boat. Jesus wanted to sit in the boat a little way out from the shore and preach to the people while they stayed on land. Peter agreed, helped Jesus into his boat and rowed a few strokes out into the lake. Then Peter and all the others listened as Jesus preached to them.

When Jesus had finished, Peter must have picked up his oars to row back to shore, thinking that was the end. Instead, Jesus told him to row out further into the lake and let down his nets into the water. Peter was surprised and said so. 'We've fished all night and caught nothing!' But then Peter wisely said, 'But at your word I will let down the nets.' Peter knew that Jesus was no ordinary man. Almost immediately the fishing nets were full of fish, so full, in fact, that they began to break and the boat began to tip. Peter shouted to his partners James and John and his brother Andrew to come and help. There must have been a frenzy of activity as the other boats raced through the water to help Peter haul in that miraculous load of fish.

Peter fell down on his knees before Jesus. He now knew beyond doubt that Jesus was the Messiah, the son of God. So he humbly said to Jesus, 'Depart from me, for I am a sinful man, O Lord.' Peter recognised that he was not worthy to be noticed by God's son, never mind to receive such a wonderful miracle. But Jesus comforted him, 'Don't be afraid' and then went on to say, 'Follow me, and I will make you become fishers of men.' It took Peter no time at all to make up his mind at that invitation. He and the others brought the huge catch of fish back to shore and left it with their families to sell. Then Peter, Andrew, James and John followed Jesus, wanting more than anything to be with him.

Peter spent the next three years listening to Jesus' teachings and watching him performing miracles. Peter's training time must have been exciting, although it was difficult too. Peter got things wrong and sometimes Jesus had to correct him. Peter also struggled with his fears and lack of faith, but through each of those times, he learned more about God and his promises. After Jesus' death and resurrection, Peter relied on that training to be a leader and preacher to the early Christians.

Priscilla and Aquila (Early first century A.D.)

Priscilla was born into a Jewish family in Rome. When she grew up she met her husband, Aquila. Aquila had moved to Rome from Pontus, by the Black Sea. He too was a Jew. That mattered because not long after they were married, the Roman Emperor Claudius passed a law in A.D. 49 that required all Jewish people to leave the city. So Aquila and Priscilla packed up and moved to the city of Corinth.

Corinth was a busy place with connections to seaports on either side of the city. Lots of goods passed through the city creating wealth for many. In the midst of the city, Priscilla and Aquila set up their tent-making business. In Roman times tent-making was more than just sewing tents for people to live in. They worked with all types of fabrics, even leather, to make items such as draperies and decorative hangings. It required both artistic skill and strong hands. After some time had elapsed, another tent-maker came to town and asked to join their thriving business. His name was Paul.

Paul, a scholarly Jew, had been converted to Christianity and sent by God on missionary journeys around the Roman Empire to preach God's Word. When he arrived in Corinth he was looking for a place to stay and a way to pay his expenses. He became good friends with Priscilla and Aquila who invited him to stay in their home. We aren't told whether Priscilla and Aquila became Christians through Paul's preaching or before they met him. But the couple was very eager to become part of the new church that Paul had begun, even hosting it in their house. So it worked out that Paul, Aquila and Priscilla worked together for the next eighteen months in the tent-making business and in the church. Aquila had the gift of evangelism, so he helped Paul as they shared the gospel in the city. But their preaching upset the city leaders and soon Paul was hauled before the Roman Proconsul Gallio. Gallio listened to the Corinthian complaints and then impatiently told them that no Roman law had been broken, so Paul was set free. But Paul knew it was now time to move on.

Paul went to Syria next and Aquila and Priscilla accompanied him. Together they travelled, plying their trade and preaching the gospel. After Syria they went to Ephesus. But here Paul met with more fierce opposition and he moved on once more. However, Priscilla and Aquila decided to stay and Paul thought that was a good idea. He knew that the couple would encourage the Ephesian Christians in their faith through their example and teaching.

Not long afterward a man by the name of Apollos arrived in town. He was a Jewish Christian from Alexandria and eager to worship with the Ephesian church and preach to the Jews in the synagogue. The small congregation welcomed him and encouraged him to use his excellent speaking skills. But as Priscilla and Aquila listened to Apollos they became concerned. Apollos had been taught about Jesus but there were some things he didn't understand. But instead of correcting him in public, they invited him back to their home. Both Priscilla and Aquila remembered all that Paul had taught them. So they were able to kindly teach him correct Christian doctrine. Apollos listened carefully and learned so that he could then begin his own missionary journey to preach the gospel.

While there are many women mentioned in the Bible, not many are named as teachers the way Priscilla was. However, God uses both men and women to teach his Word as we will see in the following chapters. So let's begin a journey through history to meet some of the bubbling fountains that God chose to preach and teach his Word.

The Family Tree

When we read the New Testament we often think that it contains the full account of the beginnings of the Christian church. And while the Book of Acts tells us a great deal about the apostles much more happened. We know this because lots of people at that time also wrote about the church. These books are like history books, with dates and events as well as who lived and what they did. Let's see if we can sort out the various accounts to better understand what happened way back then and why it matters.

Apostolic Age (A.D. 30–100)

Let's begin with the Apostles. The word apostle means someone who was sent out on a mission. Jesus chose his apostles from those who followed him while he was on earth. He taught them and trained them during the three years they travelled together. What was Jesus training them for? To become the leaders of the church after Jesus' death, resurrection and ascension into heaven. They were given instructions to preach the gospel to all the nations and that's what they began to do. Peter preached at Pentecost[1] which resulted in the conversion of 3,000 people in Jerusalem. That didn't go unnoticed by the Jewish leaders and soon they were busy arresting the Apostles to stop them from 'turning the world upside down'[2] with their preaching and healing.

Paul was also considered an apostle because he too had met with Jesus, although not in the same way other apostles had. After Jesus had returned to heaven he miraculously appeared to Paul as

---

[1] Acts 2:14-36
[2] Acts 17:6

he was on his way to persecute Christians in the city of Damascus. Jesus turned Paul's life upside down. Paul then became one of the leading apostles, preaching throughout the Roman Empire, establishing churches, and writing many letters of instruction to those churches that would later become part of the Bible.

The apostles taught the early church what Jesus had taught them. They had the full authority from God to speak because their message had come straight from the Son of God himself.

Early Church Fathers (A.D. 100 – 370)

As time moved on, the apostles died. Some were killed by angry Jewish leaders or Roman ones. But that didn't stop the church from growing. The more the Roman emperors tried to stop Christianity from spreading, the more it spread. New church leaders were needed after the apostles died and those who had been taught by the apostles' were chosen: men like Clement of Rome, taught by Peter, and Ignatius of Antioch, a student of John. These men taught the Word of God with authority. This authority was necessary because some people were already teaching wrong doctrines.

The Gnostics and the Arians

There were two groups in particular who tried to change the gospel as it had been preached by the apostles. The Gnostics tried to tell the Christians that their bodies were evil and only by learning 'a special knowledge' could they be saved from their sin. The Arians, on the other hand, were busy telling people that Jesus wasn't really the Son of God, but just a great preacher and teacher. Both these groups were wrong and declared heretics, people who deliberately teach wrong doctrines.

In the midst of these difficulties inside the early church, there were major problems outside to worry about too. Christians stood out from the rest of the people in the Roman Empire: they worshipped only one God, welcomed everyone whether rich or poor, and showed that they loved each other by sharing what they had. Roman leaders were worried that if Christians refused to worship all the Roman gods, their gods would become angry and all Rome's wealth and peace would disappear. So they began to persecute the Christians. They blamed the Christians for any natural disaster or civil unrest and arrested them, took away their property and even killed them for entertainment. The early church suffered a great deal, yet the Christians refused to turn from the truth of God.

Soon the role of the preacher and teacher in the church became very clear: refute wrong doctrine by teaching God's Word accurately to the people and encourage the faithful to remain true and obedient to God regardless of their circumstances. And with each succeeding generation, God raised up preachers and teachers to do just that.

By the fourth century the persecutions had come to an end with the Emperor Constantine. He adopted Christianity as the official religion of the empire, which now stretched from Britain to Egypt. So the church had peace from outside persecution, but the importance of preaching and teaching had not changed. Each generation still needed to hear God's Word.

John (we don't know his last name) was born in 349 in Antioch of Syria. John was very bright and became a pupil of a well-known pagan teacher, Libanius. Much to Libanius' disgust John converted to Christianity around the age of twenty. He studied theology and served as an assistant to Bishop Meletius for a time. But then John decided to become a monk and live in the desert where he spent his time praying and memorising the entire Bible. When he returned after seven years, he was ordained first as a deacon and then in 386 as a priest. John was an excellent preacher and his preaching quickly attracted people to the church in Antioch where he was becoming known as Chrysostom, the 'Golden Mouth' preacher.

Church Mothers?

We have mentioned the Church Fathers, but what about the women?

While women were, and are, forbidden by God's Word to be ordained as bishops or deacons, they still had an important place in the early church. During this time in history, most women married and had children. There were few opportunities for women to have careers outside their home at that time. So most often women served God as wives and mothers. Her 'job' was to encourage her husband and help him in his work as Priscilla helped Aquila. She also taught her children. But how did that help in the early church?

Many people today think that being a mother isn't very important. But let's have a look at what a mother does. A mother is our first teacher. She teaches us how to behave, how to be respectful, how to make friends. She also teaches us how not to behave and disciplines us when we are careless or rebellious. Our mothers don't have a classroom where her children sit in a row. Instead, she teaches during meals, while we are helping around the house or riding in the car. She might speak softly or loudly depending on our behaviour, but she is always looking to teach us what we need to know to become successful adults. The things we learn as a child stay with us for the rest of our lives.

Mothers in the early church also taught her children about God. She read the Scriptures to them and explained what they meant. She instructed her children to serve God first, urging them to come confess their sins and come to faith. The early Christian family was surrounded by a hostile Roman culture that hated Christians. So children would only learn about the true God from their parents and in the church.

The names of most of the mothers in the early church were never written down, but God knows who they were. However, we do know of at least two women.

Macrina the Elder: mother of Basil the Elder and grandmother of Basil the Great, Gregory of Nyssa, Peter of Sebaste and Macrina the Younger. These three grandsons became bishops in the church and were effective preachers and teachers. Her granddaughter, Macrina the Younger, was noted for her teaching ability among women. All of them were taught by their grandmother.

Monica: mother of Augustine whose writings have had such a profound effect on the church through the ages. Monica prayed faithfully for her son for years to become a Christian.

Golden Mouth
Antioch, Syria A.D. 387

John pushed through the noisy crowd barely aware of the cold wind as he made his way home to the bishop's house. All about him, stones flew through the air and people waved sticks and shouted. Then the cry echoed in the narrow streets, 'To the praetorium!' and the crowd began to surge forward. John ducked into a doorway to prevent being carried along with them. After a few minutes, when most of the mob had passed by, he was able to thread his way through the remaining streets and make it safely inside the grey stone house attached to the church.

As soon as John had hastily shut the door behind him, he heard Bishop Flavian's exasperated voice asking, 'Whatever are those foolish people doing?'

John was a newly ordained priest and assistant to the bishop. He had just returned from visiting an elderly man who was dying. 'They're rioting,' he replied with disgust. 'I was almost caught up in the mob. They seem to be angry about some new tax law and they are heading for the praetorium. I hope the prefect is able to defend himself and his home. That mob is very angry.'

The elderly bishop shook his head in sorrow as he eased himself into a wooden armchair. 'Foolish children,' he muttered. 'Where will it all lead?'

'I can tell you exactly where it will lead,' John snapped back, pulling up a stool for himself to sit at his bishop's feet. John looked much older than he was. Prematurely grey and balding, with his long face ending in a grey beard, he could have been much closer to his bishop's old age. But John didn't lack energy or opinions.

'If they do any damage to the prefect or his home, they'll have the wrath of the emperor to face. Just because Antioch is a leading city in the empire, doesn't mean the emperor will ignore a rebellious mob.'

'Let us pray it doesn't come to that,' the bishop replied. 'Meanwhile tell me how Marcus is doing.'

John's prediction turned out to be right. The mob damaged the prefect's house, and pulled down and broke the statues of the emperor and members of his family. The rioting lasted for three hours, until the prefect, who had escaped the mob, marched in with his soldiers and dispersed the tiring crowd. As the rioters slunk off to their homes, they left behind damaged government buildings and shops along with the defaced and broken imperial statues. As soon as the ringleaders were arrested, the prefect sent a messenger to Constantinople to inform the emperor himself of the treasonous actions in the mob.

Meanwhile at the bishop's house, plans were also being made.

'John,' Bishop Flavian called down the corridor. 'Come here, please.'

John came rushing into the bishop's room, thinking he was unwell. But instead he found the elderly man wrapped in his winter cloak with a packed canvas bag by the door. 'Where are you going?' John asked. 'And in the middle of February. It's Lent. Why would you travel now?'

Bishop Flavian held up a thin blue-veined hand.

John closed his mouth and stood quietly.

'I'm going to see the emperor.' Flavian explained. 'I need to get to him before the prefect's messenger, so I can plead for our people. Perhaps I can convince him to have mercy on our city instead of condemning all to death for the actions of a few people.'

John shook his head. 'I should go,' he replied. 'I'm younger and more fit. You're too old to make such a long journey. It's 800 miles away, and it's snowing!'

'No, you are needed here, John. The people need their priest to preach to them, to face them with their sin and also to give them the comfort of God's mercy. Meanwhile I'll try to squeeze some mercy out of the emperor. I'll take servants with me who will help and protect me on the journey. You stay and do your job here.'

So the bishop began his long journey while John prayed for his safety and the success of the mission. Meanwhile, the leaders of the riot were being executed one by one. Then the prefect turned his attention to the city council leaders. He had them arrested and their families thrown out of their homes because the prefect said they should have kept the city in better order. John was appalled and began to think about the sermons he should preach to the people.

A very subdued congregation filled the church that Sunday. The prefect had closed all the theatres and racecourses, so almost everyone decided to go to church. John looked out at them from the pulpit and sighed. He was ready to thunder at them for their foolish and dangerous behaviour but he could see they were already repentant. No one was boasting about their part in the riot and no one was acting with self-righteousness just because they had not participated. They were all very frightened and hung their heads in shame. The emperor held the power of life and death and all he needed to do was sign the warrant and every citizen in Antioch would be killed within days.

So John spoke to them about God's mercy, emphasising that God is the one who forgives sins and gives new life. He said that there was something worse than being executed at the emperor's command. If they were without God's saving grace then they would face an eternity of suffering in hell. But if they would call on God, he would hear them and grant them the mercy they didn't deserve. John finished his sermon by telling the people about Bishop Flavian's mission, urging them to pray for his safety and success.

As the weeks passed and Pascha grew nearer, all of Antioch waited in fear for the emperor's decision. During that time John continued to preach God's Word, challenging and encouraging the people. At last the messenger arrived from the great city of Constantinople with the dreaded reply.

To everyone's great relief, Bishop Flavian had convinced the emperor to pardon the city. There would be no massacre. Instead, the great city would lose its status as the capital of Syria and the honours that went with it. All the theatres and racecourses would be permanently closed, and they would still have to pay the taxes that had started the riot in the beginning. A grateful congregation gathered in the church on Pascha morning.

John stood up and said, 'I shall begin with the same words I spoke in the time of danger. So say with me: May God be praised, Who enables us this day to celebrate our festival with so light and joyful a heart. May God be praised, Who is able to do exceeding abundantly above all that we ask or think!'

* * *

Ten years passed as John ministered to the people in Antioch. He preached almost daily as well as studied and wrote books for both the clergy to study and laypeople to read and understand how God wanted them to live. John assumed he would remain in Antioch until the end of his life. But in October 397 something happened to change his life's work.

A message arrived for John from Asterius, the governor of Syria, asking him to meet him at the Martyr's Chapel just outside the city walls. John was puzzled by the request, but assumed the great man had some private business he wished to discuss with him as a priest. It was late in the evening, but the city gates were still open as John walked through them to the stone chapel built into the hillside nearby. The governor and a few soldiers were waiting outside the chapel and further down the road John saw a carriage with some restless horses. Not suspecting any treachery, John quickened his pace to greet the governor.

Suddenly the soldiers surrounded John, and before he could ask what was happening, the soldiers rushed him over to the carriage and lifted him in. As he stumbled to the bench seat, the governor was pushed in behind him and the door slammed shut. With a sharp command to the horses the carriage began to move. His heart racing, John's first thought was to wonder why he and the governor were being kidnapped. Fear and panic gripped him as he peered out the window to see more soldiers coming out of the woods to surround them as the carriage raced down the stone road.

But the governor smiled as he leaned back comfortably in his seat opposite John. 'Don't look so worried, Father John. No one means you any harm. I'm acting on the emperor's orders. He has decided that you are to be the next Bishop of Constantinople. We're taking you to that great city now.'

John leaned back into the coach seat, his head in a whirl. 'But why like this?' he asked.

'Because the emperor wasn't sure that you'd accept the honour and he didn't want to give you the choice. Besides, you are so loved by the Antiochian people he was afraid of another riot if he told them ahead of time that you would be leaving them. So you should take all of this as a compliment.'

John wasn't so sure about that, but he kept his opinion to himself. There was no point arguing when he was already on his way and surrounded by a whole company of soldiers. If this is where God intended him to be, then he would go.

After the long journey, John arrived in the imperial city of Constantinople set beside the gleaming blue Sea of Marmara. The carriage entered through the grand golden arch and drove through streets lined with high columns and statues.

John stared out at the beautifully carved and decorated stone buildings. Some even had gold domes gleaming in the sunlight. Constantinople was a rich city. Everywhere there were people from many nations walking about the streets. Many were dressed in silks and satins and followed by servants who carried their goods. But John also saw ragged children in doorways and beggars sitting near the markets in hopes of getting a few coins.

The coach stopped before the magnificent stone Great Church that stood across from the equally magnificent emperor's palace. John was helped out by a young deacon who ushered him to the bishop's house next to the church. John stared in dismay as he walked through the house followed by the deacon and several servants. The marble-tiled floors shone brightly and yards of brightly coloured silk draperies hung around the rooms. Gold and silver candle sticks and dishes stood on beautifully carved wooden furniture. Finally John could stand it no more.

'Where did all this stuff come from?' he demanded.

Surprised, the deacon answered, 'It all belongs to the bishop.'

'Do you mean the last bishop spent the church's money on all of this?' John asked, his anger beginning to grow.

Wide-eyed and worried, the deacon nodded.

'It will all have to go,' John announced. 'Sell it all and give the money to the poor.'

That was just the beginning. John discovered that the important people in the city expected the new bishop to give lavish dinner parties just as the last one had done. He angered them when he told them, 'No more parties!' Then he decided to meet with the bishops in the surrounding area and found that they too were spending the church's money on luxuries for themselves. So he put a stop to that. He looked into the financial ledgers and realised that very few proper records had been kept, so he appointed a new accountant with strict instructions to keep a good portion of the money to be given to the poor. Finally he met with all the priests, one by one, to find out what they were teaching the people each Sunday. To his surprise he found that some didn't bother to teach God's Word or help the sick and weak in their congregations. So he reorganised the priests, placing the faithful ones in the churches and giving the others administrative work to do. By the end of his first six months as bishop, John was very unpopular with the clergy and the ruling class. But that didn't stop him from reforming the church.

On Sundays he preached in the Great Church to large crowds. In his sermons he called on the people to give up their love of riches and luxuries and focus their love on God.

'You need to spend your time in worship and prayer, not on feasting and entertainment. You must use your money to care for the poor, the widows and the orphans.'

The people loved to listen to John's preaching because he spoke so well, but his message disturbed them and they often left the church grumbling.

One person in particular was disturbed. His name was Eutropius and he was the emperor's right-hand man. Eutropius had been born a slave, but through cunning behaviour and the help of friends, he had risen to become a consul and the most powerful man in Constantinople next to the emperor. He had even been the one who had suggested that the emperor make John the bishop, thinking that John would be so grateful to him that John would do whatever Eutropius asked him to do. But very quickly he discovered that John's first loyalty was to God and his church. Their biggest disagreement came over the issue of sanctuary.

The word sanctuary means a place of worship and a place of safety. Church law said that if someone was in danger or even if he had committed a crime, he could come into the place of worship, the church building, and be safe, where no one could harm him. He would be allowed to stay for a short time until either the danger had passed, or negotiations with the proper officials had been made. Eutropius objected to this law because many of the people he hated and tried to have killed came to the church for sanctuary and Eutropius couldn't touch them. But the more Eutropius argued with John, and even with the emperor, about the issue, the more John pleaded with the emperor to respect the church law. And then suddenly Eutropius needed sanctuary himself.

Eutropius had become very arrogant, thinking he was even powerful enough to tell the empress what to do. That was his big mistake. She became very angry with him and complained to the emperor who immediately stripped Eutropius of all his power and had him arrested. In a panic, Eutropius broke away from the soldiers as they escorted him from the palace and ran to the Great Church for sanctuary. He ran across the stone floor and straight up to the altar, where he pushed aside the sheer veil, fell to his knees and wrapped his arms tight around one of the pillars. He was weeping and shaking when John found him there.

John stood by the altar and looked down at the once powerful man. Eutropius looked up at him and pleaded, 'You will give me sanctuary, won't you?'

John could hardly believe his eyes or his ears. Here was the very man who hated the law of sanctuary now wanting to use it. But even though John might have been tempted to deny Eutropius' request, he knew what he must do. John nodded to the trembling man and then marched out to face the angry crowd that was gathering outside the church.

Shutting the large wooden doors of the Great Church behind him, John stood on the stone porch where everyone could see him.

'Kill Eutropius!' the people shouted.

'Release him in the name of the emperor,' the captain of the palace guard ordered.

John understood the people's anger. Eutropius was an evil man and had used his power to hurt and kill many people over the years. But John stood firm, even against the emperor's orders and protected the man who had been his enemy.

He held up his hands to quiet them all and then said, 'You know the law. Anyone who enters the Great Church and asks for sanctuary will receive it. I will protect Eutropius with my life, if I must. Leave him to me and I'll speak to the emperor about what is to be done with him.'

Slowly the cries and shouts began to cease as John convinced them to go home. The people respected their bishop and trusted him to do the right thing; even the captain of the guard listened to John and returned with his soldiers to the palace.

The next day was Sunday and the Great Church was packed with the faithful as well as with curiosity seekers who wanted to see the mighty Eutropius on his knees at the altar. John sat in his bishop's chair while the deacon read the scriptures and the choir sang. Then he began to preach.

'Vanity of vanities! All is vanity! says the preacher in Ecclesiastes, and here is a prime example.' John began, pointing to Eutropius. 'Where now is the pomp and circumstances of his consulship? Where are the gleaming torches? Where is the dancing and the festivals? Where are the garlands and the curtains of the theatres? Where is the applause? They have all vanished away like dreams at daybreak, like spring flowers that wither in the summer heat. Vanity of vanities! All is vanity!'

The people listened, at first with pleasure to see the hated Eutropius so humbled, but then John shifted his focus to his congregation, challenging them not to think that their wealth or position counted with God. See how Eutropius, who had everything, now had nothing.

'All these things will pass away. Only what you do for God will matter. Stop spending your money on fine clothing or jewels. Stop wasting your time on entertainment. All of this only makes you proud and lazy. Think about how God wants you live! Seek him and his kingdom.'

When John finished, the people were silent. They had heard their bishop and they went home thinking carefully about what he had said.

Beware! False Teachers

John had planned to protect Eutropius according to the law, but Eutropius decided to sneak out of the Great Church one night and escape from the city. A short time later he was caught by the imperial soldiers and executed on the emperor's orders.

John's life didn't get any easier in Constantinople. He continued to insist that serving God came even before serving the emperor and empress. But the empress didn't see it that way. She decided to erect a statue of herself outside the Great Church one Sunday morning. The noise from the workmen putting it in place and then the trumpets to celebrate its arrival disrupted the worship service. John angrily rushed out of the church and denounced the empress for her vanity and for disturbing the worship of God. After that John's career and life were in danger. Eventually John was stripped of his office of bishop and exiled from the empire. Accompanied by soldiers, he was made to walk over 600 miles to his prison. He never arrived, dying of exhaustion within a few miles of his destination.

Preaching God's Word did not guarantee an easy life at any time in history. Since humans are born sinful, even as babies we are God's enemy and hate his truth. Until our hearts are changed by God, we don't want to have anything to do with God. So it is no surprise that the Bible tells us to expect persecution if we follow Jesus. Opposition from outside the church is to be expected. But more importantly, the church also needs to be aware of those inside the church who try to lead people astray. Jesus himself warned his disciples to look out for false teachers. As was mentioned in chapter three, heretics surfaced in the church almost from the beginning and they kept popping up in one form or other throughout history.

You remember that the Gnostics believed that you needed a special knowledge to be saved and the Arians taught that Jesus was not God's son, just a great teacher? Well, now we are going to meet two more groups that taught wrong doctrines and tried to cause problems in the church.

Pelagianism

Pelagius lived and taught in Rome in the fifth century. He thought that everyone was born good and without sin. He believed this because he said that when Adam and Eve sinned they only hurt themselves and none of their descendants were affected. As a result, he said that people had the free will to choose to do good and follow God's commands or choose to do evil and reject God. God's grace was not needed to make the choice, only to help a Christian grow once they had chosen God.

Pelagianism appealed to a lot of people because they liked to think they were good and could make all their own choices. So this heresy quickly infected the church. But just as quickly, preachers and teachers spoke against Pelagius's teachings. The Bible clearly teaches that Adam's sin did infect all of humanity and each one of us is born with sin already in us. We cannot choose to do good without God's grace.

Manichaeism

A man called Mani was born in the third century in Persia, now called Iran. Mani, struggling with how to explain evil, came up with a complicated theory that he said was taught to him by God. He believed that there had been a struggle between good and evil even before creation and in that struggle God lost parts of himself. These parts, or points of light as he called them, were captured in our human bodies. Mani then designed a religious programme to help free these parts of God (good) from the body (evil). His plan included only eating certain foods, only being allowed to work at certain jobs, not getting married or, if you were married already, not having children. This seemed like a good plan to people who thought they should work hard to be saved from their sins. But the Bible teaches that we can't earn our salvation, that it only comes from God, through Jesus' death and resurrection.

Mani's teachings also appealed to people who liked to study and discuss philosophy and science. They often met to have debates and discussions, exercising their minds. A man called Augustine was one of those who liked nothing better than to participate in these learned conversations. He was born in A.D. 354 in northern Africa, in what we now call Algeria. During the third and into the fourth century this area was part of the Roman Empire. Augustine was a bright young man and his parents eventually sent him to Carthage to study rhetoric and law. While he was there, he met the Manicheans for the first time. He also met a young woman and fell in love with her, but he didn't marry her. Instead she became his concubine, a sort of second class wife. Her name is not recorded in any of the historical texts, but since Augustine loved her we will call her Cara, the Latin word for beloved. They lived together faithfully and had a son.

Augustine's mother, Monica, was a Christian. She was very upset with the way her son was living and prayed for him daily. Because Augustine knew his mother was displeased, he decided to stay in Carthage and become a teacher. However, after several years he was ready for a change and decided to try living in Rome where he would have a better chance of meeting influential people. Augustine had ambitions to move up in the world.

Learning How to Speak: Rhetoric Classes

If you were a boy who was good at school in ancient Rome, then your father might pay extra for you to go to a rhetoric school. (Sorry, girls, we weren't allowed!) You would be assessed in the Ludus (primary/elementary school) and the Grammaticus (grammar/high school) for the gifts to go on to higher education. But higher education was only for the wealthy. Rhetoric classes were offered in special schools, each founded by a teacher well-known for his teaching ability. The key thing was to be taught by the teacher with the best reputation, which could be in any of the major cities in the empire. So at the age of fourteen you could be off to travel to Athens, Carthage or even Antioch.

But what was rhetoric? Rhetoric is another word for public speaking, but it wasn't just a speech class. A man by the name of Quintilian came up with the Five Rules for a powerful speech.

1. Inventio (invention): learning how to develop your argument.
2. Dispositio (arrangement): learning how to arrange or organise your arguments in the best way.
3. Elocution (style): deciding how to present your argument using figures of speech and other techniques effectively.
4. Memoria (memory): learning and memorising your speech so you could speak without notes. This also included memorising famous quotes and facts to be used in impromptu speeches.
5. Actio (delivery): practising your speech with hand gestures, tones of voice and making sure your pronunciations were correct.

These five steps were repeated over and over with each speech that you would research, write, memorise and then deliver until your teacher was satisfied you couldn't improve anymore. And what would all this speechifying practise prepare you for? To be a lawyer, who defended or prosecuted in court, or a politician, who was elected to the Roman senate. Both these professions were considered the best jobs in the empire. They could make you famous and usually lots of money.

The Restless Heart

Carthage, North Africa A.D. 383

The last rays of the setting sun lit up the sky as Augustine stood at Carthage's harbour. All around him, sailors bellowed orders while loading and unloading their ships and the sea birds screamed overhead. Standing close by him on one side was his mother, Monica and her young serving girl. On the other side stood a younger woman, Cara, and their eleven-year-old son, Adeodatus, who kept trying to wander closer to the shore when his mother wasn't looking.

'Mother,' Augustine spoke loudly, over the noise of the harbour. He didn't look at her, focusing his attention on a sailing ship docking at the wharf and absently stroking his black beard. 'It's getting too late to sail for Rome today. We'll wait until tomorrow when the winds are more favourable.'

Monica gave a sigh of relief. 'Then I'll have time to go to Cyprian the Martyr's Shrine to pray for our safety. Will you meet me there?'

Augustine now shifted his gaze to his son, motioning him to come back. 'Of course. See you in the morning.' Then he reached over to give his mother a quick kiss on the top of her curly grey hair.

As Augustine watched Monica walk away with her serving girl carrying her bag, Cara spoke. 'I thought we were sailing tonight. Why are you delaying?'

Without turning around Augustine replied, 'We *are* going tonight. As soon as mother is out of sight, we'll board the ship and be on our way.'

'Augustine!' Cara reproved him softly. 'That's very unkind. Your mother loves you.'

Augustine shrugged and motioned them to follow him. 'She loves me too much,' he replied. 'I don't need her following us to Rome and preaching at us all the while. Christians can be very tiresome.'

The voyage across the Mediterranean Sea to Rome was an uneasy one. Not only did Augustine suffer from sea sickness, but his conscience troubled him too. By the time they landed at Ostia, a city just south of Rome, Augustine was feeling unwell. The three made their journey along the stone road to Rome but by the time they arrived Augustine was very ill with a high fever. Cara was in a panic, not knowing who to ask for help.

'Find Alypius,' Augustine managed as he collapsed on the bed at the inn, his darkly tanned face shining with sweat. 'He'll be with the Manichee community.'

'Your mother says they are heretics,' Cara replied, carefully covering Augustine up. But he just pushed aside the covers and moaned. So she decided to do as he said.

Bewildered by the strange bustling streets, Cara clutched the arm of her son as they wandered up and down the paved roads of the city. People from many nations filled the street, but many didn't speak the Latin dialect that Cara and Adeodatus did. At last they were able to find directions to the address that Alypius had given Augustine some time before. A servant led them into the atrium with a bubbling fountain sparkling in the sunlight and surrounded with plants. Cara and Adeodatus sat down on stone benches nearby and waited anxiously while the servant disappeared into the house.

Alypius, dressed in a pale blue woollen toga and leather sandals, rushed into the atrium. 'Cara, I didn't know that you had arrived. How lovely to see you. But where is the great teacher himself?' he asked with a laugh.

'He is very ill,' Cara replied, her dark eyes full of tears. 'Please come. He's at the inn and I don't know what to do.'

Alypius's smile faded. 'Ill? That's terrible. We will go at once.'

Alypius then turned to his servant who was standing close by and gave orders to summon the doctor and several servants to come with him to carry Augustine back to his villa.

They made quite a parade through the busy streets with Alypius leading the way and two servants carrying a stretcher with a delirious Augustine tossing on it. Cara and Adeodatus walked at the end carrying their bundles of clothing and other personal items.

The doctor came daily to treat Augustine and slowly he began to recover. After a few weeks he was able to leave his bed, and then he was eager to explore their new city. Rome wasn't so different from Carthage. It was just as big and noisy. There were many churches but there were just as many pagan temples too, all beautifully constructed of marble and stone. At first Augustine wondered where he would set up his new school in such a large city. But Alypius, through his connections in the Manichean community, found them a small villa to live in where he could start his school. Soon Augustine's reputation for speaking and teaching grew and students began to arrive.

'Roman students are much better behaved than Carthaginian ones,' he remarked to Cara one afternoon after the last of the students had left.

'Hmmm...' Cara muttered. 'More respectful, but not any better at paying for their lessons.'

Augustine sighed. 'True. I'll remind them again tomorrow.'

Then Cara changed the subject. 'Alypius sent a servant this afternoon to invite you to another banquet this evening. He said that it would be good for your career to attend. I said that you'd likely be there.'

Augustine's face lit up. 'Yes, indeed. I wonder who he'll introduce me to? Maybe I won't have to teach non-paying students for much longer!'

Augustine arrived at Alypius' villa that evening eager to spend time with his Manichee friends, although he had to admit he was having doubts about their beliefs. His friends were all learned men who enjoyed discussing philosophy and solving the problems of the world. Augustine found these discussions invigorating; in the same way some men enjoyed the competition in sport. But when it came to discussing their religious beliefs, Augustine found himself becoming dissatisfied with the Manichean religion. He was finding the Manichean arguments less and less convincing or even logical. But he thrust aside all those thoughts as a servant showed him into a dining room brightly lit with torches and already full of men reclining on couches around a table full of food. The room was also full of discussions and debates.

'Augustine, my friend,' Alypius called out above the noise as he rose from his couch. The voices subsided a little as some looked around to see the new arrival.

Augustine smiled at those he knew as he made his way to Alypius at the far end of the table. Settling himself comfortably on a couch beside Alypius, he accepted a silver goblet of wine from a servant and raised it to his host by way of thanks. Then after taking a deep drink, he looked around, noting more carefully who was present.

'Augustine,' Alypius interrupted his thoughts. 'I'd like you to meet Symmachus, a Prefect of Rome and a sadly misguided pagan,' he finished with a teasing laugh. 'But we value his company anyway.'

Augustine looked across the table to an older Roman man sitting next to Alypius and nodded a greeting. Over the noise of many voices, Augustine managed, 'I'm very pleased to meet you, Prefect.'

Symmachus smiled briefly and nodded. 'We must speak later,' he replied. 'I've been hearing good reports of you and your school. Alypius tells me you are a talented speaker too. I just might have a position for you that you would find pleasing.'

Augustine felt his heart beat a little faster. This was exactly what he had hoped for and it was difficult not to start asking Symmachus questions about the position right away. Later, after many of the guests had gone, Augustine's patience was rewarded. Symmachus told him that the young emperor, who had chosen to live in Milan, was looking for a court professor of rhetoric. Augustine was to come to Symmachus' villa the next day to discuss the position to see if Augustine was right for the job.

Later Augustine burst into his bedroom where Cara was already asleep and shook her awake. Pushing her long dark hair out of her eyes, she struggled to sit up.

'What's happened? Is Adeodatus ill?'

'No, no,' Augustine replied with a grin. 'It's something good. If all goes well tomorrow, we could be moving to Milan and I could be the emperor's court professor!' He sat down on the bed and gave Cara a joyous hug.

Still muddled with sleep, Cara pushed him away. 'What are you talking about?'

Augustine then launched into a long description of the evening. 'Just think,' he finished, well pleased with himself. 'A court professor at the age of thirty. How's that for the son of a minor African government official?'

Everything worked out just as Augustine had hoped. That autumn, after being in Rome for only a year, they packed up their belongings and headed north to the city of Milan. They travelled with a company of merchants and some soldiers, who would protect them from outlaws. Augustine was full of excitement and anticipation, as was his son. Augustine smiled fondly as he watched Adeodatus trying to convince the soldiers to let him handle their weapons. But his smile faded as he looked over at Cara. He knew she was worrying about what these changes would mean to their family. He had tried to reassure her that nothing would change his love for her.

As they travelled further and further north, they all began to notice the cold winds coming down from the mountains. They put on more layers of tunics, wrapped their feet and legs with woollen cloth and pulled their woollen cloaks tightly around them. Milan was going to be very different from their home in warm Carthage or even Rome.

After settling into the villa provided for the court professor, Augustine prepared himself to be presented to the thirteen-year-old Emperor Valentinian and his mother, the Empress Justina. Augustine pushed aside a brief wish that he could take Cara too, but since she wasn't his wife, he couldn't present her at court. Both the emperor and empress welcomed Augustine kindly and he took up his duties as the emperor's teacher.

Augustine was also keen to keep honing his skill as an orator. He was told that the Bishop of Milan, Ambrose, was an excellent speaker, so Augustine decided to attend the worship services to hear this great man preach. He planned to make notes about Ambrose's style, diction and language, but ignore the tiresome Christian beliefs his mother, Monica, held so dear.

The idea worked well. A few months later, on January 1, Augustine was invited to give a panegyric to honour the emperor at a ceremony in the palace court. Augustine worked hard preparing the speech, using some of the tips he had picked up from Bishop Ambrose, and everyone applauded him afterwards. Both the emperor and his mother were very pleased.

Augustine had planned to stop attending Bishop Ambrose's church after his successful speech because he thought he had learned everything he could about public speaking. But somehow that never happened. Augustine found himself drawn to hear Ambrose's sermons each week and actually listened to the message. Not that he wanted to become a Christian, he assured himself. He was just interested in the ideas and philosophy.

During this time Augustine's mother, Monica, arrived in Milan. She had finally followed them from Carthage, stopping at Rome for a time and then heading north to Milan when she heard where her son was now living. She wasted no time in finding his villa, eager to see him again.

'My son,' Monica greeted Augustine as he returned home from the court one evening. She gave him a hug and several kisses on his black-bearded face. 'You are looking so well. And so much the professor,' she smiled proudly. 'How far you have come, to the very court of the emperor.'

'Thank you, Mother,' Augustine replied, returning her hugs. He was relieved that she didn't complain to him about his trick of leaving her behind in Carthage two years earlier. Over his mother's shoulder he noticed Cara standing in the doorway, looking very unhappy. He wondered what his mother had said to her. He soon found out.

Monica began, 'I'm so glad to hear that you're attending worship and listening to Bishop Ambrose. He is truly a great Christian, someone who could answer all your questions, I'm sure.' Augustine was about to reply when Monica quickly changed the subject. 'But now that you have such an important position and you're investigating Christianity, don't you think you need to make another important change in your life?'

Augustine was puzzled. Change? What change would he need to make now? He wasn't ready to become a Christian just yet. There were still too many things he wanted to know and didn't understand about God. 'Sit down, Mother,' he said with an uneasy feeling. 'If you're thinking of preaching to me, I won't listen, but I will offer you some refreshment. You've had a long journey.'

Monica took the hint and sat down, watching as Augustine motioned Cara to join them. A servant brought them warmed wine sweetened with honey and some small honey cakes. Cara sat down reluctantly, watching Monica as if she might bite her. Monica glanced up at Cara with an unfriendly expression. Alarmed, Augustine began to tell the long tale of how they came to Milan and what he had been doing for the last six months in his new position. As his story finished, Monica turned to him with a fond smile.

'I'm so proud of you, Augustine. You have come such a long way from just being a teacher. And there is so much more you could achieve ...' She paused and looked over at Cara. '... if you had a proper wife. You can hardly take your concubine to court dinners or celebrations. But if you had a wife from a good family with connections to all the other great Roman families, just think where you could end up.'

Both women looked at Augustine, who took a large bite of honey cake to prevent him from answering right away. No matter what he said, one of them was going to be hurt. He had loved Cara for many years now, but he had to admit his mother was right. Since coming to Milan he had wished he had a socially accepted wife by his side. As he chewed slowly he saw the expression on Cara's face change from hope to despair, as if reading his thoughts. His mother too saw his hesitation and thought she might have persuaded him. Augustine suddenly rose and left the room, unable to face either of them.

Sometime later Augustine returned from a long walk to find everyone had gone to bed. The house steward told him that they had made up a room for Monica, who was planning to stay with them. Augustine sighed and went to his own room where he found Cara in bed crying quietly.

Before he could speak, she said through her tears, 'You want me to go, don't you?'

'Cara,' he began, pleading. He gathered her into his arms and hugged her tight. 'I love you deeply. There is no other, but my mother is right. For my career to continue moving ahead I need a proper wife.'

She nodded miserably. 'Then I must go. I'll pack tomorrow. But I want you to know I will never have another man in my life.

I will return to my parents' home and care for them. You are the only one I love. I suppose I will have to leave Adeodatus with you?' she asked.

'I can offer him so much more than you can,' Augustine replied quietly.

Again she nodded and then slid down into the bed and closed her eyes. Augustine felt miserable and guilty[1].

Their parting was the most difficult thing that Augustine had had to do thus far in his life. He felt like a part of his body had been ripped away as he watched Cara ride away on a donkey. He had paid well to give her a safe escort back to Carthage. Adeodatus was unhappy too and moped about, missing his mother. Only Monica seemed satisfied with the outcome. She began to use her time to get to know the influential families, finding out whether they had any daughters of marriageable age.

Not even the arrival of Alypius from Rome and their mutual friend Nebridius from North Africa could cheer Augustine up. The news that his mother had found a young girl from an important family to be his wife only made him feel worse. Fortunately, the girl was too young for marriage and they would have to wait a couple of years. Meanwhile, Augustine, together with Alypius and Nebridius, continued to go to hear Bishop Ambrose preach every week. And every week he came away with some answers and more questions that made him think he needed even more time to decide about Christianity. The three men discussed and debated while Monica continued to pray that God would have mercy on them and bring them to faith.

Back and forth Augustine went with his desire to understand and become a Christian. He kept finding arguments that made him doubt what he heard Ambrose teach. But then he'd hear stories about others

---

[1] Historians have several opinions about why Augustine and Cara didn't marry. Most think it was because Cara and Augustine were from different social classes, and it was illegal for two people from different social classes to marry.

who gave up successful careers in the imperial service to serve God and he would admire their courage and willingness to leave their comfortable homes and salaries. Could he do that? All he had ever wanted was to be a successful teacher and receive praise for his talent. But that had not brought him the happiness he thought it would.

One day his indecision drove him to tears so he went out into the garden to be away from everyone. The day was fair and he sat under a tree wishing he knew which way to turn. Suddenly he heard a child's voice singing out from next door, 'Take. Read. Take. Read.' Augustine sat up and looked around. On a table not far away was a codex of Paul's letter to the Romans that his friend Alypius must have left behind earlier that day. Augustine picked it up and opened it. The codex fell open at Romans 13 where he read the last sentence:

'But put on the Lord Jesus Christ and make no provision for the flesh, to gratify its desires.'

All at once Augustine felt all his doubts fall away. All the fears, questions and restlessness inside his heart and mind were replaced with a peace he didn't know was possible. At last he understood that Jesus Christ was the answer. Nothing else mattered, not his great ambitions or his comfortable lifestyle. He could hardly wait to tell his mother and his friends.

Is this the Apocalypse?

Augustine gave up a promising career in the empire to serve God. After his conversion he chose not to marry but instead returned to his home in North Africa where he eventually became bishop in the city of Hippo, known today as Annaba in Algeria. Many people must have thought 'what a shame that such a gifted man gave up the chance to be so great.' But what they and Augustine himself didn't know was that he would be a great influence on many generations of Christians with his books. Augustine focused his energy and great intellect to write books to teach others about God. His best known book is about his own spiritual journey, which he called *Confessions*. Augustine was careful to give God full credit for the gifts and abilities he was given to lead and teach God's people.

Augustine died in A.D. 430 just as the Vandals had begun to lay siege to Hippo. This Germanic tribe had migrated through Europe during the previous century. Then they crossed over the Mediterranean Sea at Gibraltar and began taking over the coastal cities of North Africa, starving many of the Roman citizens and stealing their goods. This was the beginning of a century of suffering and unrest throughout the Roman Empire.

By the fifth century the Roman Empire was no longer strong or united. Officially it stretched north to the River Rhine, east to Palestine, west to Britain and south to North Africa, but in reality it was slowly falling apart. The various tribes and peoples that the Romans had conquered in previous centuries decided to rebel. They wanted to enjoy the riches of the empire and not just pay the taxes. And so the invasions began.

Wave after wave of what the Romans called barbarians arrived ready to conquer the weakened empire: Vandals, Goths, Lombards, Visigoths, Huns and Ostrogoths, a strange sounding group of names but fearsome bands of warriors. They showed little mercy to the people they captured, either killing, beating or selling them for slaves. They burned the cities and towns and took everything of value. Then they set their own king to rule over the people. Imagine if you lived during that time, how full of fear you would be, wondering which group of barbarians would invade next and try to take control from the group already in power. Not only did the people have to endure these invasions and constantly changing kings, there were even more difficulties. The bubonic plague swept through Italy several times during the century and into the next, killing huge numbers of people. Then repeated droughts occurred and few crops could grow, so that those who survived the plague had very little to eat. And finally, heavy storms brought repeated floods, drowning people and the few crops that had managed to grow. It was so frightening that people began to wonder if these were the end times. They had read or heard read the book of Revelation that tells about the complete and final destruction of the world. They thought the world was coming to an end.

It was not, but that didn't change how much the people suffered. Many turned to the church for help and comfort, while others prayed and sacrificed to their idols and pagan gods. It was a difficult time for church leaders to provide leadership. The Roman roads, that had linked all parts of the empire at one time, had fallen into ruin, so communication was more difficult. Priests and bishops couldn't always reach the people isolated by the ravages of the wars. Churches, too, were destroyed by the invaders and their golden treasures carried off, so instead of beautiful places to worship, Christians were worshipping in tumbledown buildings and even in caves.

In the midst of all this upheaval a young man by the name of Gregory was growing up in Rome. He was born in A.D. 540 into an aristocratic family with connections in the government and the church. God protected Gregory in all the confusion of war, famine and plague. He was able to study both Roman law and the writings of the church fathers. He read Augustine and Jerome's writings. When he was about thirty-three years old he was appointed Prefect of Rome, a government position. He didn't enjoy the job and resigned within a year to join a monastery. He preferred to study God's Word instead of being a government leader. However, Gregory was noted for his fine understanding of the law and administration and it wasn't long before he was called out of the monastery to serve the church.

A Servant of Servants

Rome A.D. 578

Gregory stomped through the gate of St Andrew's monastery onto the stone road, answering Brother Porter's farewell with a growl. Then he stopped. 'Lord forgive me,' he muttered. Turning around he went back to the startled monk and apologised.

'Forgive me, Brother. It's not your fault I have to leave this place.' He gazed longingly back at the wooden buildings grouped around a stone chapel. He sighed and turned to face Brother Porter, who was smiling with relief.

'God go with you, Brother Gregory,' he said. 'Wherever you are sent.'

Gregory bowed his head. 'And may he give me a willing spirit, too,' he replied.

With a farewell wave, Gregory left the monastery once more, wearing his monk's habit and hitching up his leather satchel on his shoulder that contained a few prized books. With a heavy sigh he began to work his way up and down through the hilly streets of Rome to the Lateran Palace. After climbing a particularly steep hill, Gregory was out of breath. His strict fasting and going without sleep in the monastery had left him weak and with a painful condition of gout. He found a crumbling low stone wall by the side of the road where he sat down, grateful to give his throbbing foot a rest.

Gregory looked around at his home city. What a sad state it was in. The cobbled streets had loose stones and potholes. Many of the buildings were in disrepair. Instead of crowds of people going about their business, only small groups shuffled along here and there, looking fearful. The constant reports of barbarian attacks nearby made people uneasy and had reduced the food supply to the city. Sighing heavily once more, Gregory rose to finish his journey to keep his appointment with Benedict, the Bishop of Rome.

The elderly pope, or bishop of Rome, greeted Gregory with a kiss on his red-bearded cheek. 'Thank you, my son, for coming to our aid. I know it was difficult for you to leave your brothers at St Andrews, but there is work to be done for God here that only you can do.'

Gregory bowed his head respectfully, while biting back a sceptical retort. Instead he asked as humbly as he could, 'What would you have me do?'

'I want to ordain you as a Deacon. The church needs administrative reform. With all of the chaos created by the barbarian tribes, the terrible plague in the city and the famine outside, we have lost a lot of good men. Your experience of running your family estates when you were younger and the time you served as Prefect of Rome has given you the training to help me run the church.'

'That was years ago,' Gregory protested.

'Surely you exaggerate,' Benedict chided him. 'It has only been six years. No more excuses. You are here to serve God.'

Gregory, who chose to continue wearing his monk's habit, was ordained a short time later. Before he could do any work for the church, Pope Benedict suddenly died. The emperor appointed Pelagius[1] to be Rome's new bishop. Pelagius wasn't about to let Gregory return to the monastery. He, too, realised how valuable Gregory's gifts were in getting things done and winning friends at the same time. Pelagius had just the project for Gregory to do.

'My son,' Pelagius said one day. 'The people are suffering and I plan to do all that I can to help them. I want you to take on a building project.'

---

[1] This is Pelagius II, not the Pelagius who taught the heresy discussed on page 38.

Gregory frowned. How was that going to help the people?

Pelagius continued. 'I want to convert my family's villa into a home for the elderly. So many have died in the last few years that those who still live no longer have family to care for them. I want you to draw up the plans, hire the workmen and see that it is done quickly.'

Gregory smiled. This was a project he would take on happily. It kept him busy for over a year, until Pelagius found a bigger job for him. Summoned once more to see the pope, Gregory assumed that Pelagius wanted a report on how the buildings were coming along, so he brought the plans with him. But Pelagius waved them aside.

'Give them to your fellow deacon,' he said. 'You are no longer in charge of that project.' Puzzled, Gregory obeyed, handing the large scrolls to a young man who appeared at his side. 'Now,' said Pelagius, 'I want you to prepare yourself for a long journey. You may take some of your brother monks for company if you like, but you must be ready to leave in a few days.'

'Where am I going?' Gregory asked.

'Constantinople. As you know, the barbarians have conquered and settled into most of the land around us. Only Rome and Ravenna are still under the emperor's control. Now the Franks are threatening to lay siege to our city and our soldiers are too few to hold them off for long. I need you to plead with the emperor to send us troops to protect us. You understand government politics and you get on well with people. Go and make friends of our eastern brothers and persuade them to come and help us.'

Gregory began to prepare for the journey, even though he wasn't particularly happy about it. He knew it would be difficult to keep himself from being caught up in the busyness and intrigues in the imperial court. Setting aside time for prayer and Bible study would be challenging. So Gregory was pleased when some of the monks from St Andrews agreed to accompany him. They would help him stay focused on serving God instead of people.

The journey by sea was difficult and dangerous, but still safer than the overland route which would take them through barbarian duchies. The sailing ship hugged the coast going south and then set out east across the Mediterranean Sea. Once they had rounded the coast of Greece the ship headed north through the Aegean Sea to the Marmara Sea and the great city of Constantinople. All the while they prayed for good winds to fill the ship's sails and to escape any dangerous storms. Gregory was relieved to see the high walls of the city come into view and the several harbours full of ships.

The ambassadorial party was welcomed at the Gate of the Plateau and led through the busy streets to the Placidia Palace, the usual home of the Roman ambassador. Gregory felt a little embarrassed by the honour given to them and the fussing of the servants. He behaved graciously to the imperial party, assuring them that everything in the palace was fine and that he would present himself to the emperor the following day. But once the officials had departed, Gregory called his fellow monks together.

'I can't live with all this luxury,' he told them. 'I'm afraid I will come to like it too much. Are you willing to live as we did in the monastery, simply, in just a few rooms and eating plain food?'

They all agreed without hesitation because they too felt uncomfortable with servants to wait on them and soft beds to sleep in.

'Thank you, my friends,' Gregory replied. 'I see you as my anchored cable to hold me fast to the tranquil shores of prayer. If you see me drifting into the court life more than I should and being tossed about by the waves of secular affairs, please pull me back to renew my focus on God.'

Over the next few years Gregory did his best to become friends with Emperor Tiberius Constantine and then his son Emperor Maurice. But while they were both sympathetic to the difficulties in Rome, they had no troops to spare. Their soldiers were busy keeping the barbarians away from Constantinople. However, Gregory was always welcome at the court and in the churches to preach. He also made friends of several other ambassadors and developed a special friendship with Leander, the Spanish diplomat.

Leander was a pious man and eager to discuss theology. He persuaded Gregory to begin preaching a series of sermons on the book of Job. The sermons were well received by the emperor. His fellow monks also persuaded him to write these sermons down as a commentary for others to use. However, his preaching also caused some controversy when Patriarch Eutychius decided to challenge Gregory on a doctrinal matter.

The Patriarch wrote a book about the resurrection saying that there would not be a bodily resurrection. Instead he said a Christian's resurrected body would be like air. Gregory preached against the idea, pointing out that Jesus himself had a bodily resurrection and so would all Christians. The quarrel became very bitter, with both men claiming they were right. So Emperor Tiberius finally called them to the court to debate in front of him. After much discussion the emperor agreed with Gregory and ordered that the Patriarch's book be burned. Shortly after that the Patriarch died of an illness.

After five years in Constantinople, Gregory was recalled to Rome and replaced by another ambassador. Pope Pelagius had other duties waiting for Gregory. There were disputes among the Italian bishops that needed sorting out. Gregory was assigned the delicate job of mediating among them in the hope of restoring peace. That and many administrative issues kept Gregory busy for the next three years and away from the quiet monastic life he longed for. However, Pelagius did allow Gregory to live at the monastery while he came to work each day at the Lateran Palace. Life fell into a routine until the autumn of A.D. 589.

Gregory watched from the window of his office in the palace as the torrents of rain fell on the streets below. They had had weeks of rain and the rivers and creeks were rising steadily. He ran his hand through his sparse auburn hair. He knew many people had already moved to higher ground in the city as the Tiber River began to overflow its banks. And along with the flood waters came water snakes whose poisonous bites killed as many as the flooding.

Just then a sharp knock sounded on the wooden door and it was flung open by Peter, one of his fellow deacons.

'Brother Gregory! Come quickly! Our pope is very ill and is calling for you,' he said.

Gregory dropped his quill pen causing the ink to splatter on the document he had been writing. But rather than take the time to mop it up, Gregory rose from the desk and followed his agitated friend through the corridors to the pope's private chamber.

Pelagius was very ill, with all the signs of the plague. He lay shivering in his bed, his face shiny with sweat. He wasn't aware of anyone else in the room. The doctor shook his head and said, 'He won't last much longer. It came on suddenly and will finish quickly.'

The doctor was right. An hour later, Pope Pelagius was dead. With great sadness Gregory arranged for the funeral. He didn't know who would be chosen to be the next bishop but he hoped this meant that he could at last return to St Andrew's monastery and stay there for the rest of his life.

After the funeral, a delegation of bishops came to Gregory and asked him to be the new pope. Gregory was appalled. 'I don't want the position. Surely one of you could do it.' But they argued with him, saying he had a better understanding of the church as well as the gifts of administration.

'You know the people of Rome and their situation much better that we do. You know what needs to be done,' Peter the deacon said. Then he added, 'Even your brother, who is now Prefect of Rome, has recommended you.'

Gregory retorted. 'He's not a bishop and not entitled to make these decisions. And besides the emperor must confirm whoever is chosen. I'm sure I can recommend one of you instead of me.'

But it did no good. Gregory's brother intercepted his letter to the emperor and sent his own instead, telling Emperor Maurice that Gregory was the best man for the job. The emperor agreed. He wrote to Gregory, ordering him to obey the will of the bishops and the people. Gregory reluctantly obeyed.

At the beginning of the year A.D. 590 Gregory was inaugurated as Bishop of Rome and the head of the western part of the church. Even though this was a position he never wanted, he promised to do his best for God's glory and his church. Almost immediately disaster upon disaster began to unfold and Gregory was busy being a pastor and preacher to a suffering city.

A group of Franks invaded Rome, destroying and stealing whatever they could find. Rome had few soldiers or strong leaders so the barbarians ran freely throughout the city. Gregory stepped in, and with the help of his brother, organised the troops to repel the Franks. When the enemy was finally driven out, they left behind a damaged city. But there was no time to weep or even think of rebuilding because the barbarians had brought the plague with them and many people fell ill all at once.

Gregory called all the priests and deacons to the Lateran Palace to instruct them to go out into the city and care for the sick and the dying. He was most concerned for those who were pagans and had not heard the gospel. 'The people need to prepare to meet God and his judgement. You must tell them of Jesus' sacrifice for sin and urge them to repent. But you must also comfort those who are resting in God's grace, assuring them of their salvation.' And so they went out, preaching and comforting the people in the midst of a disease for which there was no cure.

Even as so many were suffering from the plague, a great tornado ripped through the centre of Rome, demolishing homes and churches and killing people in its path. Gregory fell on his knees before the altar in the church, pleading with God to relieve the city of all these terrible events. By the end of his first year as Pope, Gregory was exhausted. And he was very troubled.

Gregory knew that with the barbarians settling in the lands all around Rome, many of the Christians were cut off from each other. They might gather together in small groups and maybe have a priest to minister to them. These Christians needed to know that they weren't forgotten and they needed good leadership. So Gregory sat down and wrote a book on how to be a good pastor along with some sample sermons. This handbook was designed for the priests to use as they cared for their small isolated churches. Gregory then called together all the deacons in the Lateran Palace and instructed them to make as many copies as possible so the book could be distributed far and wide. Gregory called his book *Liber Regulae Pastoralis* (Book of Pastoral Care).[2]

Meanwhile, Gregory found himself unwillingly drawn into political matters. The Lombards, who had conquered and settled all around Rome, had chosen a new king, Agilulf. Along with his Bavarian princess wife Theodelinda, he was planning to capture the cities of Rome and Ravenna and become the sole ruler of Italy. Naturally, everyone turned to Castus, the military governor of Rome, to defend them. However, Castus had a problem. His soldiers hadn't been paid by the emperor and were threatening to leave their posts and go home. Everyone was in turmoil. They turned to Gregory for help.

'What do you mean that Castus can't get his soldiers to defend the city? Do they want to die at the hands of the Lombards, too?' Gregory demanded of the group of deacons and local leaders. No one answered.

Gregory paced up and down in his sparsely furnished chamber while the group of men stood about waiting for him to speak. He was angry. Angry at the Lombards for daring to threaten his

---

[2] This book is still used today in some seminaries as an instruction handbook.

beloved city. Angry at Castus for his poor leadership. And he was angry that he was called away from church matters to handle this political crisis. 'Show me the map,' he ordered. One of the deacons swiftly produced a large scroll which he unrolled on the wooden table in the room. Bending over it, Gregory studied the location of the Lombards in the north and tried to think of what strategy they could use to defend the last two great cities in Italy.

'They will try to cut us off from each other,' he said, 'since we are separated by so much land. We will need to send troops to the centre and then watch what Agilulf does. Whichever city he moves toward first, our soldiers will need to attack them from the rear, diverting them from that city.'

'But what about the soldiers?' another deacon asked. 'They say they won't fight.'

'Oh, yes, they will,' Gregory replied in a determined tone. 'Gather them in the square outside the palace and I'll speak to them personally. They have a duty to God and to the people.'

The next day Gregory spoke to the troops and rallied them to fight the Lombards. The same day, Gregory sent out messages to the outlying fortresses that help was on its way. Then he set about appointing new commanders to lead the troops.

Unexpectedly, the Lombards held their position rather than advancing on Rome. Gregory heaved a sigh of relief. But the lull was short. A new duke in the south, Ariulf, began to gather his army to invade. His first move was up the middle, cutting off Rome and Ravenna from each other. And then he advanced to Rome. The Roman troops that were supposed to attack from the rear were too few against so many barbarians. Ariulf and his army arrived at the gates of Rome.

Gregory was ill when the invaders arrived, but he left his sickbed to meet Ariulf at the gate to plead with him to spare the city. Ariulf said he would consider leaving them alone if they paid him and his soldiers well enough. Gregory knew he had no authority to negotiate with the barbarian duke, but he also knew that it would take weeks to get a message to the emperor and receive an answer back. That would be too late. So Gregory went to the church's treasury and gave it all to Ariulf. Gregory reasoned that the money would be of no use to the church if Ariulf invaded and killed everyone. The amount was enough, so Ariulf agreed to leave Rome in peace, but not before the two men became friends. Ariulf himself had fallen ill during the negotiations and Gregory visited him, suggesting a milk diet as a remedy. Ariulf recovered and was grateful. Gregory could have let him die, but instead Gregory had won over the barbarian duke with kindness as well as money.

What a Mess

A.D. 600–1300

Gregory's contact with the Lombards didn't end with his treaty with Ariulf. Once the immediate threat of invasion passed, Gregory set about negotiating a treaty with King Agilulf and Queen Theodelinda. That took much longer. The emperor was not pleased with Gregory's interference in politics. But as Gregory pointed out, he was in the middle of the problem while the emperor was safe in Constantinople and occupied with other matters.

However, it was more than politics that concerned Gregory. He was also concerned about the souls of his enemies turned allies. He began to send out missionaries to some of the barbarian towns to preach the gospel to their kings and queens. Six years later, both Agilulf and Theodelinda converted to Christianity and they encouraged their people to do the same.

Gregory also sent a missionary further afield, to Britain. His name was Augustine, named after Augustine of Hippo. He began his mission work in the town of Canterbury, where he built a church and a monastery, and began to preach to the Anglo-Saxon people and their king, Aethelberht. The king, already married to a Christian Frankish princess, accepted the gospel readily and gave Augustine and his fellow monks permission to preach freely among the people.

Many historians view Gregory as the one who changed the role of the pope. Up until his time, the pope was simply the Bishop of Rome who was considered to be the leading bishop of the western churches. The Patriarch in Constantinople had a similar position in the eastern churches. But because Gregory became so much a part of the government when there was no one else to lead, a precedent was now set. A precedent is best described as an event that happens for the first time and then becomes 'the way' or the pattern for doing it again. And that's what happened with the papacy over time. Gregory had made political decisions as well as church decisions, so therefore the popes who came after him thought they could do the same. They ignored the fact that Gregory only did it because of his particular situation. This led to a lot of other changes and controversy in the coming centuries.

By 800 the papacy was very involved with the kings of the various countries that were forming in Europe. When Pope Leo III ran into trouble, he called on Charlemagne, King of the Franks, to come and help him. Charlemagne, who had been busy conquering most of Europe, turned his army around and marched them to Rome. Faced with a threatening army, Pope Leo's enemies decided to leave him alone. The pope was so grateful to Charlemagne that he crowned Charlemagne Emperor of the Roman Empire, or as the position came to be known, Holy Roman Emperor. This meant that now the emperor and the pope were a team, one taking care of the political life of the empire and the other the spiritual life. Or at least, that was the idea. It didn't quite work out that way. And just to make it all the more interesting, the emperor, or at this time, empress, in Constantinople said 'Hang on a minute, I'm in charge of the empire.' If times had been different the empire could well have erupted into war between the two rulers and between the pope and patriarch. However, each part of the empire had its own internal problems and external threats to deal with. Constantinople was fighting off the Muslims on their eastern borders and Rome was dealing with another king, Henry III of Germany, and his constant interference in church appointments. Neither had the energy to deal with this new problem. So, while the eastern part of the empire grumbled at the western part, they both chose to focus on their difficulties at home.

The final split between both the empires and the churches came in 1054. The western church sent a delegation to Constantinople to discuss the theological differences over their interpretation of the Nicene Creed. This was a debate that had been going on for several centuries. The meeting was poorly handled on both sides; church leaders lost their tempers, said outrageous things to each other and then excommunicated each other. A very sad way for Christians to treat one another. Over time the two churches failed to reconcile with each other and remain apart even today.

During the next 300 years, the behaviour of church leaders in the west went from bad to worse. The position of pope became far more political than spiritual. So if a young man wanted to do well during these centuries, he went to a monastery and studied hard to become a priest. Then he did his best to get on the good side of his bishop who could promote him up to higher positions in the church. Maybe even one day, if he knew enough of the right people, had important relatives and played the political games, he could become a pope. Sadly, it all had very little to do with his relationship with God or his ability to teach God's people. And just as bad, instead of being concerned with right doctrine and studying God's Word, the church leadership was only interested in the people's obedience to their every decree. So they began to use the word heretic in a different way. Instead of calling someone a heretic for teaching wrong doctrine and trying to mislead God's people, a heretic was now someone who disagreed with the church leaders. They used the threat of excommunication to keep people in line.

Excommunication was a serious matter in medieval times. Not only did it mean a person could not come to church or receive the sacraments, it also meant that no one could speak to him, sell him food or goods or even allow him to remain in their town. It was like a death sentence. Only those who were very brave would even risk the anger of church leaders and the threat of excommunication.

So where were the faithful Christians during this time? Did the true church die out completely because of the mess the church leaders were making of the church? Of course not. God is not defeated by selfish, rebellious people. There were many faithful Christians who continued to worship God and pray for the reform of the church. God heard their prayers and even when things seemed at their worst, God called some to preach his Word and risk excommunication and even death.

One such man was John Wycliffe, who lived, taught and preached in Oxford, England. He spoke out about the corruption he saw in the church and called for reform. He wanted the church leaders to give up all their wealth and political intrigues and return to preaching God's Word. He taught his students and his congregation the true doctrines of the church.[1] They in turn told others and so the gospel continued to spread even when the church leadership continued to serve themselves instead of God.

A few years before Wycliffe died in England, John Hus was born in a small village in Bohemia, now part of the Czech Republic. He loved music and fine clothes and had plans to live a comfortable life, but God had a different plan in mind for John.

---

[1] You can read more about John Wycliffe in *Guarding the Treasure: How God's People Preserve God's Word,* (Volume 1 of Defenders of the Faith) by Linda Finlayson.

Search the Scriptures!

Bohemia 1390

John's rich tenor voice filled the small wood and stone church. He sang the first verse of the final hymn and then the choir of men and boys joined in, their music ringing out about the rafters. In the silence that followed, the priest pronounced the benediction and then began the procession down the centre aisle. The precentor smiled at John, nodding with satisfaction, and signalled for the entire choir to follow him down the aisle.

As John passed some of his school friends, he heard one whisper, 'Not bad for a farmer's boy.' John grinned and continued out of the church.

Once outside in the damp autumn day, the precentor turned to John and said, 'We'll miss you here in our little church. Your voice has served God well.' Then he handed John a small cloth bag with a few coins in it.

John took the money and slipped it into his leather purse fastened around his waist under his choir robes. 'Thank you,' he replied. 'I'll miss you and the music, too. I hope I can still sing in churches in Prague.'

'I'm sure you will. I have written you a letter of recommendation to show the precentors there,' he said.

The priest also came up to John. 'Be sure to look up Christian when you get there. I've written to tell him that you're coming. He's already completed his first degree,' the clergyman said proudly, as if he had been the one to achieve such success. Most people in the town of Prachatice took credit for their local lad who was doing so well in the big city. 'I'm sure he'll help you settle into the university.'

Eighteen-year-old John nodded and thanked them with a smile on his narrow face, all the while wishing they'd let him go. He still had to say goodbye to his parents in the next village and then pack up his few belongings. He could hardly wait to be on the road to Prague.

When John arrived in Prague, he walked about the streets gawking at all the beautiful stone buildings with their red tile roofs. The crowds of people seemed to jostle him at every turn and he received various insults in different languages for standing in the way. One German-speaking young man even waved a knife in his face. Thoroughly shaken, John was relieved to finally stumble into the university courtyard clutching his knapsack.

After a few inquiries, John found Christian and introduced himself to the young man who was wearing a plain black university gown over his blue doublet and hose. Long pointed blue shoes peaked out from under the gown's hem. John couldn't help admiring Christian's clothing. One day he hoped to have enough money to dress that well. Meanwhile he was very conscious of his own shabby brown doublet, patched hose and farmer's boots.

'Welcome to Prague,' Christian greeted him. 'So how do you find the big city?' he asked with a teasing smile. 'Exciting?'

'Dangerous,' John replied. 'Some German threatened me with a knife just because I was in his way.'

Christian's smile faded. 'Ah, yes. You might as well learn about surviving in Prague.' He put his arm around John's shoulder and started to lead him down the street as he spoke. 'Prague is seething with rivalries and you must be careful not to get caught up in them. Students come from all over to our great university: Saxons, Czechs, Poles, Bavarians, Bohemians like ourselves, and Germans.' Christian almost spat out the last word. 'Watch the German students carefully. In fact, avoid them if you can. They are arrogant and always spoiling for a fight, and, as you now know, they carry weapons. So don't go out alone and you should carry a knife for protection.'

John looked around with a worried expression.

Christian slapped him on the back and said, 'Don't worry. If you take precautions and spend your time studying instead of socializing about the town, you'll be fine. Now let's find some food for you and then on to your lodgings. I'm sure you'll make friends quickly.'

As it turned out, John never had much money to go out in the town. He found some work in the city churches singing in the choirs, but to his bitter disappointment not all precentors remembered to pay him. So there were times during the first year when all he could afford for his dinner was some cooked peas which he ate with a bread spoon. As much as John wanted to devote himself to his studies, he had to find another way to earn the money he needed. So he hired himself out as a servant to the masters of the college. While it was physically tiring, this gave him a rent-free room and dining privileges with the other servants. Then he could study after his serving work was done.

John studied very hard and soon found a close friend in Jerome, a brilliant scholar. They spent many hours discussing philosophy and theology. They both wanted to earn enough degrees to eventually teach in the university, although they differed on one point.

'Why do you want to be ordained as a priest?' Jerome asked one day over a meal of cheese, bread and beer. 'Do you have a calling?'

John paused before taking a deep drink from his wooden tankard. 'No, not particularly,' he replied. 'But I do want the big house and regular salary that comes with the position.'

'But what about the preaching and the pastoral work? I wouldn't want to do that. Becoming a master at the university is enough for me.'

John shrugged and pushed away any uneasy thoughts by changing the subject. 'When I earn my master's degree, I plan to give a big feast. Will you come?'

Jerome nodded and raised his tankard. 'May we both be rewarded for our efforts.'

By the time John was twenty-four, he had earned two degrees, his bachelor's degree and his master's degree. As a result he was offered a master's position at the university to teach. He was very pleased with himself and paraded around in his academic robes and hood trimmed with fur. He gave the feast he had promised Jerome and invited his fellow masters of the college and some close friends. It cost a great deal, but John wanted everyone to know of his achievements and celebrate with him. Besides, he counted on his university salary to help pay the debt and the additional money he would receive when he was ordained a priest. He was sure that he had reached his dream of living in comfort with lots of fancy clothes while pursuing an academic life.

However, something unexpected happened to change his life. During that six years of study, both John and Jerome came across some books written by the English professor and theologian, John Wycliffe. Being good scholars, they knew that all ideas should be investigated to see if they were true. So they read what Wycliffe had to say about the Scriptures and the practice of the church. And to their great surprise, both men found themselves interested in what Wycliffe wrote, which led them to begin a more careful reading of the Bible than they had done before. The more they studied the Scriptures, the more the Holy Spirit gave them understanding about what they were reading. Gradually John came to realize that his ambitions were all wrong in God's sight. God changed John's heart and mind so that he now understood that his purpose in life was to serve God and his church. Jerome, too, experienced the same heart change.

'I need to know more,' Jerome declared one day in 1399. 'I've decided to go to Oxford University in England and learn more from Wycliffe's writings and his followers.'

'I wish I could go with you,' John replied. 'But I think it's more important for me to stay here and teach the students what we have learned. They need to make studying God's Word a priority so they can know the truth. I need to speak out against some of the church leadership for their abuses and teaching wrong doctrines to the people. We need to train young men to serve God and not themselves.'

So they parted, each intent on serving God in a particular way. The next year John was ordained as a priest, a calling he now took more seriously than he had planned. Instead of sitting back and enjoying his extra income, he gave away much of his money to those in need. He also refused to take the 'extra' money that people offered him for his priestly services: baptisms, funerals, hearing confessions or presiding over the Communion service, as well as all the tithe money. He was appalled to discover it was common practice to pay the priest extra for what was really part of his job.

Jerome returned from England in 1401 with copies of Wycliffe's books that he had written out himself. He began to share them with John and other masters of the university.

'See here, in this book, Dr Wycliffe has said everyone should have the Bible in their own language, the one they speak and understand the best,' Jerome pointed out to John.

'Then it would make sense to also preach to them in their language instead of Latin,' John said.

These were new thoughts, and they excited John. So when he was asked to be the rector of Bethlehem Chapel in Prague, he was able to put them into practice. The chapel had been founded ten years before as part of a nationalist effort to minister to the people in their own language. John was prepared to preach in the Czech language as the founders had planned.

He moved into the rather plain-looking building, using the second floor flat as his new home. Dumping his bags of books and his university robes on the bed, John stepped out from his room into the wooden pulpit that was mounted half way up the wall. From here John could see the vast area below and the wooden gallery opposite the pulpit, all of which could hold up to 3,000 people. On the plain plaster walls, below the high windows, were framed frescos of biblical stories and famous churchmen. He felt overwhelmed with the honour and the trust that he had been given.

'Almighty God, please give me the wisdom to teach your people and the courage to speak your truth, in season and out,' he prayed.

John settled into his new home, writing his sermons and his lectures. He divided his time between the chapel and the university, teaching and preaching to as many as would listen to him. In the chapel he preached in the Czech language and each week the chapel was packed to capacity with people hungry to hear God's Word. In the university, he continued to teach in Latin, as was required, but his students were just as happy if he slipped into Czech in their discussions afterwards. Most of the other college masters began to follow Wycliffe's teaching too, which angered some church leaders. However, John acquired a new friend, who encouraged him to keep speaking the truth, at least at first.

John, now thirty-one, went to meet the new Archbishop of Prague in the episcopal palace as part of his duty as a priest. A deacon showed him into the Archbishop's study that contained a small fireplace with a brightly burning fire, a few shelves of books and a large wooden table that served as a desk along with two chairs. A man, younger than John, with golden hair and a soldier's build turned to greet John.

'Master Hus,' he said with a broad smile. 'How pleased I am to meet you. I have heard much about your teaching and preaching.'

John returned the smile, bowing politely, causing his long beard to brush his academic gown. 'Welcome, Your Excellency. I trust we will work well together.'

'Ah, that is exactly what I wanted to speak to you about. Please sit down.'

Once they were settled in chairs set near the fireplace, Archbishop Zbynek began. 'As you know, I'm a trained soldier, serving our King Wenceslas since I was fifteen. Now that he has helped me to become archbishop I need some advice on how to serve the people in Prague. I don't have a theological education so I was hoping that you would consider becoming my advisor, helping me make good decisions for the church.'

'Certainly,' John replied, troubled that his superior in the church knew so little about God's Word. But he was happy to have an opportunity to teach the archbishop some of Wycliffe's doctrines and be an influence for good.

John liked the young archbishop and they met often to discuss doctrine and church matters in Prague. He especially appreciated this new friendship because he missed Jerome, who had decided to study in other universities in Europe and spread Wycliffe's teaching wherever he could. John also took on a translation project. The Bible had been poorly translated into the Czech language and John spent several years revising it. Now the language was clearer and easier to understand. Every time he preached, he urged the people to read the Bible every day.

'Search the Scriptures!' he preached. 'Check to see if what I preach is true. Hide God's Word in your heart and obey it. God's Word is the path to life.'

He also preached at the synod meetings, but on a different theme. Here he preached against the corruption in the church: the selling of indulgences, clergy taking the tithe money for themselves, priests who ignored their parish and chased after political favours. 'Love the Lord your God with all your heart and with all your soul and with all your mind'[1] he thundered out to the assembled bishops. Some, in turn, shuffled uncomfortably in their chairs. But the archbishop nodded, approving John's sermon.

---

[1] Deuteronomy 6:5

John preached at the synod two years later, again urging the clergy to 'stand, therefore, having girded your loins with truth'[2]. Many nodded, agreeing that changes had to be made, and especially that every priest and bishop should study to know God's truth. John, along with many others, were excited to see that changes were possible in the church and continued to press for reform. Within a year changes began, but not for the better.

In 1408 the friendship between John and the archbishop began to fall apart. John wrote some angry letters to Archbishop Zbynek when some of the reforming preachers were suddenly arrested. Zbynek reacted by accusing John of a sinful attitude and asked someone else to preach at the Synod meeting that year. John continued to complain that priests who disobeyed God's Word were left alone, while those who preached the Gospel were persecuted.

In the midst of this personal problem, both men knew there were greater problems that needed to be addressed. Back in 1378 the Great Schism began in Rome. Instead of one pope, two popes were elected, each claiming they were the 'real' pope. This caused great confusion. Who should the church listen to and obey? Bishops, priests, kings and the people all began to take sides, some even using the confusion as an excuse for battles. By 1409 the cardinals of the church had had enough of this and called a council to meet in Pisa to decide who should be the real pope. After much discussion all that was accomplished was to elect a third man, Alexander, to be pope. Now the church had three popes!

In Bohemia, King Wenceslas IV remained quiet about which pope he would support, but not Archbishop Zbynek. He chose to recognize Gregory XII as the real pope. So the king decided to have a quiet word with Pope Gregory. King Wenceslas' reign had been full of troubles. He and his brothers, also kings of neighbouring countries, didn't get along and at one point Wenceslas was imprisoned by one of his brothers. So King Wenceslas asked Pope

---

[2] Ephesians 6:14

Gregory if he would recognize him as the greater king and give him the title of Holy Roman Emperor. Gregory, who supported Wenceslas' brother, said no. King Wenceslas was very angry and called in his archbishop.

Zbynek bowed low to the red-headed king glaring down at him from his throne. He was worried, but ready to defend himself.

'I have made a decision. I will be supporting Pope Alexander and so will you.'

The archbishop was about to reply "no" when he looked around at the armed guards. So he tried to reason with the king. 'Your Majesty, Pope Gregory is living in Rome, in the papal palace as the pope should. The others are not. How can they claim to be chosen by God?"

The king leaned down and said with a menacing voice, 'I say that Alexander is the pope. Will you argue with me?'

Casting another quick glance at the soldiers and then at the angry king, Zbynek made a choice. "No, your majesty. Of course, you are right.' Then the archbishop, who hadn't really meant what he said, asked the king a question. 'That Master Hus is stirring up the people against all the church leaders with his preaching of Wycliffe's reforming ideas. Shouldn't we ask the pope for permission to stop him?'

King Wenceslas thought for a moment. "Hus is our problem, not the pope's. You deal with him."

Zbynek bowed and began to formulate a plan as he rushed away. He decided to disobey the king and ask Pope Gregory for a Bull to ban the reading and preaching of Wycliffe's works and stop the reformers from preaching. That should silence his former friend.

A few months later the letter from the pope arrived, much to the archbishop's delight. He announced immediately that Wycliffe's books were now banned. When John heard, he wrote a stern letter to Zbynek and then read it out on Sunday to his congregation. In response, the archbishop demanded that everyone surrender all books of Wycliffe's that they owned to be burned, and then he excommunicated John Hus. But John's followers were not about to let him be treated that way and they formed an angry mob that tried to attack the archbishop. Frightened, Zbynek fled the city of Prague to a place a safety. A few months later the archbishop died unexpectedly, but that didn't stop the persecution of the reformers.

A month later Jerome burst into John's flat at the Bethlehem Chapel with the latest news. 'John, you've been summoned to Rome by the papal curia to answer charges of heresy. And if you don't go they'll excommunicate you from the entire church.'

John closed the book he had been reading and sighed. 'I thought King Wenceslas had written to Rome and told them to leave me alone.'

'He did,' Jerome replied, clearing some books off a chair to sit down. 'But then you preached that sermon against the church selling indulgences. That made the king angry because you criticized the pope he supports and, I suspect, that he gets some of the money from those indulgences in return for his support.'

John pounded the desk, making the books jump. 'Is there no end to the greed and corruption?'

'Maybe you should be making plans to find a safe haven,' Jerome suggested.

'My place is here and at the university, teaching the truths of Scripture. Should I abandon the job God has given me to do?'

But within a year John had to do just that. When he refused to go to Rome, the entire city of Prague was punished. Pope John, who had replaced Alexander when he died the previous year, placed an interdict on the city. That meant that the city was sealed off from the rest of the country. No one could bring in goods to sell, or take goods out. Priests were forbidden to conduct worship, baptise or bury people. It caused a great deal of suffering, so much so that John decided he had to leave the city to set it free from the interdict. With much sadness, John Hus packed up what he could carry and walked through the city gates, wondering where he would go and what would happen next.

Too Many Changes
1410-1532

God still had plans for John Hus, although he only had a few years to live. He remained in exile for two years and then, when he was offered safe passage, he finally agreed to attend the Council of Constance to defend his teachings. This council had been called to finally resolve the many popes question and they elected Martin V, whom everyone accepted as the only pope. However, now that the church was united once more, they were very anxious to silence anyone who criticized the church. When John appeared before the council they asked him who was the head of the church, wanting him to recognize Pope Martin V. Instead, John told them Christ was the head of the church, not the pope, or cardinals or any other human being. That sealed John's fate. In anger they declared him guilty of heresy and John was burned at the stake the following year. He died singing praises to God in the Czech language.

It took two more years to settle the Great Schism. But that brought no peace to the church or to Europe as a whole. John's followers in Bohemia continued to spread the message of the gospel throughout the country. They were called Hussites, and they were anxious to see the church leaders reform their ways and return to teaching only what was in the Bible. Some people joined the Hussite movement who also wanted political freedom for Bohemia along with church reform. Once King Wenceslas died in 1419, an all-out revolt began between the Hussites and the king's brother, Sigismund, who fought for the pope and the church. After many years the Hussites won.

Meanwhile other changes were taking place in Europe. The invention of the printing press by Johan Gutenberg changed communication in the fifteenth century. Books could now be printed more quickly than handwritten books. They were also cheaper and easier to distribute. New ideas and ways of doing things began to spread just at the time when more and more people were pleading for reform in the church.

God chose Martin Luther as the person to bring it all to a head. Martin was a monk, a priest and a university professor. The more he studied the scriptures, the more he came to realise that many of the church teachings were wrong. Over the centuries the church had slipped into error, telling people that they were saved from their sins by their works such as attending worship, making confessions and giving their money to the church. These are all good things that people should do, but these works do not save anyone from God's wrath. Worst of all, people had the impression that they could live as they pleased the rest of the time and so long as they confessed their sins before they died, they would go to heaven. Salvation only comes through accepting God's grace through his son Jesus Christ, who died in the place of sinners. But they were ignoring all those passages in the Bible. They had forgotten that those who follow Jesus should live their lives to please him and not themselves. It was a very sad time in the life of the western church.

As Martin rediscovered these truths he experienced God's saving grace in his own life and he began to tell others. When Martin heard that a priest by the name of Tetzel was travelling around selling indulgences for Pope Leo X, he spoke out against the sales. Martin had no plans to leave the church. He only wanted to correct the wrong teachings and practices, and bring them back in line with the teachings of Scripture. But the church leaders, particularly Pope Leo X, didn't see it that way. They saw Martin's criticisms as dangerous. They were convinced that they would lose the power and wealth that they had accumulated through the sale of the indulgences, and that was more important to them than following God's Word.

After a number of years, Martin was ordered to appear before Emperor Charles V, the dukes of the Holy Roman Empire and the church inquisitor. Martin was given the choice of recanting his beliefs or being excommunicated. Martin chose excommunication because he believed that God's Word was more important than a priest or a pope's wrong teachings. Not only was he excommunicated, but he was threatened with a death sentence. But that was never carried out. Instead his patron, the Duke of Saxony, protected him. He gave Martin freedom to preach, teach and write in Saxony, and soon his influence was felt all over Europe. A new church was forming called the Protestant church. It was made up of people who protested against the wrong teachings of the Catholic Church.

The word *catholic* means universal or something that everyone is part of. Up until the time Martin Luther's writings caused the split in the western church, that was true. Everyone in the west belonged to the Catholic Church regardless of their nationality or language. Everyone was baptised into the church as infants, attended worship, listened to the priest, married in the church and were buried by the church when they died. Now that was no longer true and it was a very upsetting turn of events for most people in Europe. All the ways they were used to were changing.

Some welcomed the change because they were convinced they must obey God's Word rather than the words of men. A few saw the changes as an excuse to behave badly. They decided they wouldn't obey anyone: not the pope, the king or their local priest or pastor. But a great many people found the changes very difficult. They were used to relying on the Catholic Church to tell them how to live, just as their parents, grandparents and many generations before them had done. They became angry that Protestants wanted to change it all. Lastly, there was the group of church leaders and others who truly believed the Catholic Church's teachings. They were not only angry, but they did something about it.

Remember how the word 'heresy' changed its meaning? Instead of heretic meaning someone who taught wrong doctrine, it had come to mean someone who opposed the Catholic Church. Well, that last group of people began in earnest to hunt down and persecute those who called themselves Protestants because they were now called heretics. Protestants had to be very brave. They had to worship in secret, be careful who they spoke to about their faith and be prepared for possible arrest and even death. It was a time of great suffering for the church and it lasted for several centuries.

While Protestants, both rich and poor, were facing this persecution, they needed to understand what they were being persecuted for. They needed clear teaching from the Bible about what they should believe and why. God raised up a man to do just that. His name was John Calvin. He was born in 1509 in France. Since he was clever and his father was well off, John was educated at the best schools in Paris, Orléans and Bourges in both theology and the law. When John was in his early twenties, he was converted and became a Protestant. Not a safe thing to do, as he soon found out. But God was going to use John's clever mind to help those who were suffering for the gospel's sake.

'All I want is a quiet life'
Paris 1533

A loud knock sounded on John Calvin's university room door. He was sitting by the window reading a book, which he closed with a sigh. Why couldn't people just leave him alone to pursue his studies.

'Enter,' he called out reluctantly.

His friend, Nicholas Cop, thrust open the door. With a broad smile on his bearded face, he bowed with a flourish in the doorway. In spite of his dismay at the interruption, John laughed at his friend's antics.

'What do you want now?' John demanded with a look of mock severity on his thin face.

Nicholas stepped into the room and announced, 'You are looking at the next rector of the university.'

John leapt up and clapped Nicholas on the back. 'Well done, my friend. When will you give your inaugural lecture?'

'In a few weeks' time.' Nicholas's face became sober. 'And I will have much to say that will be unpopular,' he continued as he sat down on the other chair in John's room. 'I'm hoping that you will give me your opinion on the lecture before I give it?'

John agreed even though he knew it was dangerous. He and Nicholas, along with some friends, were convinced that Luther was right about the reformation of the church. John had to agree that there was no better time to call for those reforms in Paris than with Nicholas' lecture. Church leaders, university masters and civil magistrates would all be there to hear what Nicholas had to say.

Several weeks later, John sat in the university chapel watching Nicholas climb the steps to the pulpit. Dressed in his academic robes, Nicholas opened his notes and began to speak. John watched the audience more than he watched his friend. At first they were interested, listening carefully, but then the mood began to change when Nicholas called boldly for reform of the church. Some of the university masters began to get angry and a few even walked out. John began to worry about what would happen next.

Within a few days, news from the Sorbonne leaked out. Nicholas was going to lose his new position and maybe even be arrested. As soon as John heard this, he rushed to Nicholas' lodgings and urged him to leave the city.

'You must leave. No good will come of you spending time in prison,' John pleaded. 'You are a gifted scholar who can teach. Go to Basel where it is legal to speak openly about God's Word.'

Nicholas agreed and packed up a few belongings before making his goodbyes. 'I will miss you, my friend. Be sure to put your excellent legal brain to good use for the gospel's sake.'

John knew he would miss his friend, but was relieved that Nicholas was able to leave Paris safely. And that, John thought, was the end of the matter. But it wasn't.

A few days later John met Michel, Nicholas' brother and a court physician, on his way back to his lodging. Michel was out of breath and upset. 'Don't go back yet. The soldiers are there and there's talk of arresting you because of Nicholas. They think you helped him write his lecture.'

John's heart began to beat fast. He knew he had to get out of Paris quickly. 'I'll wait until they've gone and then I'll get a few of my belongings to take with me. I'll need a disguise so I can pass through the city gates without being noticed.'

Michel nodded. 'Farmers are always coming and going from their farms outside the city. I'll try to get you some old clothes. But don't follow Nicholas to Basel. Our friend Louis has already gone home to his village to minister to his congregation. Why not hide out there? It's protected from persecution by the king's sister.'

Later that day John slipped into his rooms to quickly pack up some clothing and books. He was distressed to see his papers and letters strewn all over the floor and his books knocked off the shelves. But there was no time to worry about it.

By the time the sun was setting, John was walking toward the city gates. He wore the patched doublet, leggings and cloak that Michel found for him even though they didn't smell very nice. No one stopped him as he left the city of Paris and began his journey south.

Several days later, John arrived in the town of Saintonge in south-western France. Lutheran sympathisers were allowed to live in the province of Navarre because the king's sister had declared she would protect them and not even the king dared to argue with her. John knocked on the door of Louis du Tillet's cottage and received a warm welcome.

'Come in, good friend,'Louis greeted John. 'I heard about Nicholas's lecture and his flight from the city. Did you have to sneak away too?' he asked with concern, handing John's cloak to his manservant. Peering at his face, Louis continued, 'You don't look well, John. Please, sit down.'

John sank gratefully into a well-upholstered chair by the fireplace and closed his eyes, letting the warmth of the fire thaw out his chilled body. After a moment he smiled wearily at his concerned host. 'I'm on the run, Louis. I need a place to hide for a while.'

'Ah, now I see. The old clothes are a disguise. Here, have some refreshment before you tell your tale.' Louis settled down in the chair opposite John and motioned to his servant to set down a pewter tray with two goblets of mulled wine on a small table close by.

Both men drank deeply and then John began to tell his friend about the soldiers in his room, how Michel had helped him and his long journey. Louis listened intently until John ran out of words and sank even further into his chair.

'You may stay here as long as you need to,' Louis assured him. 'God has graciously provided me with a powerful patron in Queen

Marguerite of Navarre, who is a Protestant. Nevertheless, the Sorbonne may send spies to look for you. May I suggest that you use another name while you stay here? That should keep you safe.'

John nodded, trying to think of a good name to use while his aching body kept reminding him he needed to rest. 'I'm very tired. After I sleep, we will think of a name.'

Louis agreed and showed John a room for him to use while he visited. John barely noticed anything except the bed he fell into and went to sleep almost immediately.

The next morning John woke up to the sun shining on his face and birds singing in the garden. His body still ached and his chest was sore, but he got up anyway. While he dressed he came up with his new name: Charles d'Espeville. Charles was a common name and Espeville was a village that John had once visited. It would do.

After breaking their fast together, Louis showed John his library. Amazed, John wandered around the room that was full of books and manuscripts collected from all over Europe. Here were Bible commentaries, philosophers and much more from centuries past. Calvin grew more and more excited as he looked at the books.

'How wonderful! May I spend time in here? I've some writing projects that I had in mind to begin but ... well, you know the story.'

Louis laughed. 'Of course you can. This is the best place for your hide away. What do you plan to write about?'

John gazed thoughtfully at the shelves before he answered. 'I think I should first work on a book about what a Christian should believe. There have been so many changes in the church in the last few years that people don't know what is right doctrine and what is not. Some say Luther is right, some say the Catholic Church has always been right, and others just make up doctrines to suit themselves. We need a book that sets down clearly what the Bible teaches and not what this man or that tells us.'

Louis nodded approvingly. 'A fine idea. Many in my congregation need to have a clearer understanding of God's Word. With your lawyer-like mind, I know you can explain it all clearly.' He paused. 'Don't forget to come out of the library every now and then to eat and sleep,' he teased. Then he left John alone with the books.

After a year of studying, writing, and then more studying and more writing, John was well on his way to finishing his *Institutes of the Christian Religion*. He decided to show it to Louis for his opinion.

'Well done,' Louis said, as he turned the last page of the manuscript. 'I think you have covered all the important topics: the Law of God, the Creed, the Lord's Prayer and the Sacraments of Baptism and the Eucharist. And you have shown how the Bible, the teachings of Augustine and other fathers of the church are true.'

'I'm still not done with it,' John replied. 'There are parts that I think can be clearer, but I'm glad you think it is worthy of reading.'

'Indeed it is. But don't spend too much time adding this and that to the book, or you will never publish it. All those who are being persecuted for their faith will surely want to read your book soon, to understand clearly what they might be dying for.'

John nodded, a serious look passing over his face. 'Yes, the king has certainly been persecuting Protestants ever since the Affair of the Placard happened last October.'

Louis nodded his agreement and then both men went silent, remembering when the first reports had come from Paris. Some over-enthusiastic reformers had printed out placards with slogans against the Catholic Church and its leaders. Then at night they pinned up the placards all over the city of Paris and even in the king's palace. King Francis had been furious and immediately ordered the arrests of every known Lutheran sympathiser. Since then many were put in prison and some had been executed.

'I think I should leave France,' John said after a few moments. 'I want to have a peaceful life, away from the persecution.'

Louis agreed, and then had an idea. 'I know a printer in Basel who would publish your book. Why don't I go with you and introduce you to him?'

John smiled. 'I would enjoy your company, and it would be nice to see Nicholas again.'

The next week, wrapped up warmly against the cold January weather, John and Louis set out for Basel in Switzerland. They rode their horses and took two servants with them, heading north to Poitiers to visit a small group of reformed believers. Since it was so dangerous to be a Protestant in France, the congregation met in a cave outside of the city. They invited John to lead them in worship and preach God's Word to them.

As they gathered around him in the chilly cave John reflected that this was no different than what the early Christians did to hide from the Roman soldiers. As the small group sang Psalms and John taught from the Bible, the sounds echoed down the cave and into the side of the hill. Then together they celebrated the Lord's Supper where John emphasised that this was not a sacrificial mass. Jesus' death was the only sacrifice necessary for their salvation. The meal was an act of remembrance and a time to receive blessing from God.

After a few days, John and Louis left to go on to Strasbourg. On the way one of their servants robbed them of their money while they slept. Their second servant felt badly that he had not been able to stop it from happening. So he gave them the little bit of money he had in his pocket. It was enough to get them to Strasbourg and then on to Basel, where they lodged with Mrs Klein.

'Monsieur Calvin, Monsieur du Tillet, please do come in. I'm so honoured to have you stay in my home,' the middle-aged lady greeted them. 'I have rooms for you both to stay in and I'll cook all your meals and wash your clothing.'

Both men thanked her for her kindness and settled into their new lodgings.

As John continued to write and re-write his *Institutes*, Louis went out to meet with printers to find the best deal. Louis also heard the news from France from those who had fled persecution. King Francis was even more angry with the Protestants than before, and he acted without mercy. Many people died rather than give up their faith in God. John and Louis mourned the loss of some of their friends.

'You must let this book be printed,' Louis urged John one day.

John agreed, but he had one more thing to write. 'I want to dedicate this book to King Francis,' he said to Louis.

'What! Why?'

'Because I want him, and everyone else who reads this book, to know what terrible things he is doing and that he should repent. Only then will God bless him and his kingdom.'

Louis was doubtful it would make much difference, but he waited patiently while John crafted the preface of the book which began:

> *'For the Most Mighty and Illustrious Monarch, Francis, Most Christian King of the French, His Sovereign, John Calvin craves Peace and Salvation in Christ.'*[1]

When he was finished, he handed the finished copy to Louis. 'May God use this small book to instruct and guide others in the truth.'

Louis nodded his agreement and headed out the door to the printer before John decided to add something more.

By the end of that month, a number of copies of *The Institutes of the Christian Religion* were delivered to John's room. He was packing up his belongings and deciding how to carry the books when Mrs Klein came to the door.

'I'm sorry to see you leave, Monsieur Calvin,' she said tearfully, standing in the doorway.

John smiled. 'I'm sorry too, but I must go. However, I thank you for the lodgings and good food, and for allowing me to write day and night. Part of this book,' he said, as he waved his hand to the pile, 'belongs to those who helped me by allowing me to work on it. You have served your fellow believers well.'

Mrs Klein blushed and smiled. 'Where will you go from here?'

---

[1] Prefatory Address to King Francis I of France.

'To Italy,' John replied as he attempted to stuff the last of his belongings in his bag. Mrs Klein quickly came over to help him.

'Whatever for?' she asked.

'Louis suggested that we visit some of the Protestant believers there. And I want to give a copy of *The Institutes* to Renee, Duchess of Ferrara. She is the sister-in-law to King Francis and a Protestant. Maybe she will influence her brother to stop the persecution.'

'God go with you, Monsieur Calvin. And may he use your book to help many.'

Over the next few weeks John and Louis travelled through the mountains to the plains of northern Italy. When they arrived the Duchess welcomed them to her palace that stood in the centre of the city of Ferrara. The castle had been built 150 years before as a strong square fortress with tall watchtowers at each corner. John and Louis tried not to stare as they were led by the castellan through many rooms and up large stairways. Everywhere they looked they saw frescos, paintings and statues. In the long gallery artists were at work decorating the walls with frescos of maps. The Duke of Ferrara wanted his castle to feel like a luxurious palace.

At last they were shown into the Duchess' reception room in the St Catherine's Tower. The room was richly decorated with silk draperies on the walls and colourful cushions on the furniture. The short figure of Renee, Duchess of Ferrara, rose from her chair, causing all her ladies and servants to rise too. Her gown of blue satin rustled as she moved forward a step or two.

She extended her hand, with a smile on her small face. 'Welcome, Monsieur Calvin, Monsieur du Tillet. How very pleasant to greet Frenchmen from my homeland.'

Both men bowed over her hand, kissing it and then taking the chairs offered to them.

'Tell me,' she asked, 'what has brought you here?'

'I have a book for you, Your Grace,' John said. 'One that I hope you will find useful for your own spiritual life and that you will share with others.'

Louis held out a slim leather-bound volume of the *Institutes of the Christian Religion*. A young squire came forward, took the book and handed it to the Duchess. She held it carefully, opening it to the first page and read the dedication to her brother-in-law, King Francis. Then she turned the pages, taking a brief look at the various chapters. After a few moments, she raised her head, and with a solemn expression said, 'Thank you. I will read this most carefully, and as I do I would like you, Monsieur Calvin, to explain to me anything I do not understand.'

'Gladly,' John replied with a smile. He was always pleased to teach anyone hungry to understand God's Word and grow in their faith. 'Will you also send a copy to your brother in the hope that he will read it?'

'I will try,' the Duchess replied. 'But my husband might stop me. He is not a Protestant and he objects to me telling others of my faith. He might even object to you being here, although I will do my best to protect you.'

John nodded, understanding that the Reformation had torn apart families as well as countries. 'I will stay as long as God allows me,' he replied.

* * *

For the next six weeks, both John and Louis conducted private worship services for the Duchess and other believers in the city. John also had the pleasure of instructing the Duchess and they formed a close friendship. But the Duke became angry with the Duchess when one of her servant's took Calvin's teachings to heart and during morning Mass walked out protesting as he went. The Duke blamed his wife the Duchess as much as he blamed the young man. John and Louis had to hastily pack up their belongings and leave before they too ended up in prison.

'Where to now, my friend?' Louis asked as they rode their horses north to the mountains.

'I have to go back to Paris briefly to help my brother Antoine with the sale of my parents' land, but I won't stay long since it isn't safe. I plan to move to Strasbourg, where I can have a quiet life of study and writing. My brother and sister might even come with me.'

Louis said nothing at first. Then gathering his courage, he said, 'I think you should be teaching the church. You could pastor a congregation.'

John shook his head vigorously. 'No! I'm a scholar, not a priest. I can serve God just as well with my writings.'

Louis didn't reply, but he suspected that God might have a different plan for John.

* * *

Several months later John was on the road again, this time with his brother Antoine and Maria, their sister. They were heading for Strasbourg just as John had planned. With the money from the land sale in Paris, John could begin his quiet life with his sister as his housekeeper and his brother finding work in the city. However, they met a troop of French soldiers marching past them.

'Turn back!' the commander called out to them. He waved his long pike with a sharp looking axe head down the road. 'We're heading into battle not far from here. Better go back to Paris or maybe head down to Geneva,' he advised.

None of them wanted to go back to Paris. It was too dangerous for Protestants there. So reluctantly the travellers turned and headed for the city of Geneva, set by a large lake in the mountains.

'We'll only stay one night,' John announced. 'Then we will take the road north, skirting around the war zone and travel to Strasbourg that way.'

'Just one night,' he repeated to himself as he settled down in a Genevan inn for the night.

Preach the Word!

1536-1738

John Calvin didn't just spend one night in Geneva as he had planned. When William Farle, a Protestant pastor in Geneva, heard that Calvin was in town, he knocked on John's door and challenged him to stay in the city to minister to the people. John didn't want to, but William was so persuasive that John was convinced that God himself was summoning him to this task. At first the people of Geneva were thrilled to have such a great scholar and preacher in their city, but they soon changed their minds. They were surprised to find out that when John preached he expected people to listen and to change their ways. The people of Geneva liked to go to church, but they also liked to live just as they pleased the rest of the time. John spoke out about their behaviour and eventually the people had enough. After two years, they forced him out of the city. John went with a heavy heart to Strasbourg. There he finally found some time for his academic studies while he pastored a French-speaking congregation. When he received a letter two years later inviting him back to Geneva he didn't want to go. However, the Genevan Council pleaded, saying they were sorry for how they had treated him and wanted to do better. Finally John gave in and returned. He spent the rest of his life in Geneva. He pastored his church, began a seminary that attracted men from all over Europe, and wrote many books including several new editions of his *Institutes of the Christian Religion*. By 1559 he had written so much that that book now had eighty chapters full of information. John Calvin died five years later.

With the Reformation came a new emphasis on preaching. There was a keen desire to teach God's Word clearly so that everyone could understand it, not just the educated clergy or professors. Schools were set up to train men. They studied God's Word in detail along with the writings of the Church Fathers and Reformers. They also learned the languages of Greek and Hebrew in order read the Bible in the original languages. Why was that important? Because translating words from one language to another is not like doing a math equation. Words change their meanings over long periods of time. For example, when Middle English was written and spoken, the word 'seminary' meant a seedbed or a nursery where plants are grown. Then during the eighteenth century, the word came to mean a school of higher learning for girls. Today we use the word to describe an institution where pastors and priests are trained. So it's important to go back to the original languages to see how a word was used and then find the appropriate word for the present-day language. That takes a lot of time and study. However, once that has been done, then the meaning of a biblical passage becomes clearer. And the clearer the preacher's understanding of the Bible is, the better he can communicate God's Word to his congregation.

The Reformers were not trying to invent any new theology. Their aim was to return to what the apostles had taught the early church. They also relied on the commentaries written by the Church Fathers in the centuries following the early church, along with those written by faithful churchmen throughout history. John Hus, Martin Luther, John Calvin and others read Augustine and Gregory the Great's books along with their Bibles to give them greater understanding.

The invention of the printing press brought about huge changes in communicating God's Word. Books of sermons and commentaries as well as Bibles were printed more quickly and cheaply. This encouraged more people in Europe to learn to read, although not everyone had a chance to learn. The poor, who could not afford to send their children to schools or hire a tutor, continued to be restricted to hearing God's Word preached each week at church. And, it was not as easy to buy a book then as it is today. We can walk into a bookstore or order online whatever titles we want. But during the sixteenth and seventeenth centuries in some parts of Europe, owning a Bible or any Protestant material was a dangerous thing. Often their reading had to be done in secret.

At the same time that the Reformation was splitting the western church, the European nations were also changing. Larger countries were slowly forming by conquering smaller countries. While this was happening, these countries also formed along religious lines. Most of the north of Europe became Protestant, including the Scandinavian countries, the Netherlands, Scotland and some of the German states. The south of Europe was mostly Catholic: including Spain, Italy, some of the southern German states and France. In between were countries, such as England, who were still sorting out which side they were on. If you were a Protestant in a Catholic country it could be quite dangerous for you to possess Protestant literature or an unsanctioned Bible[1]. The same was true if you were a Catholic in a Protestant country. You could be imprisoned or executed. Being a Christian was not easy.

In the century and a half after John Calvin, much happened in Europe that was good for the Protestant church. England finally settled on Protestantism in the late seventeenth century with the Glorious Revolution. During the reign of William and Mary people were free to worship in Protestant churches and own their own Bibles. But that didn't mean that everyone believed in God, or went to church as often as they should have. In fact, given the choice, people tended to stay away from church, preferring to live their lives without interference from Christians. The society became very troubled. When we don't obey God's law we often don't obey

---

[1] William Tyndale, Martin Luther, William Whittingham and others were translating the Bible into the common languages of the day. These translations were not approved by the state churches in England, France and some other European countries, so they were called unsanctioned Bibles.

the civil law either. Lying, stealing and even murder becomes more common. Parents are ignored and husbands or wives are not treated kindly by their spouse. Such was the state of English society when God called several men to begin preaching, calling people back to obeying God's Word.

John and Charles Wesley grew up in England in the eighteenth century. Their father was a minister and their mother taught them the Christian faith from an early age. But it wasn't until they were adults that they were converted. Once they knew God personally, they were filled with a passion to preach to people wherever they went. George Whitefield, the son of an innkeeper, met John and Charles at Oxford University where they were all studying to become ministers. George was a very gifted speaker. As a teenager he had enjoyed performing in plays, where he learned how to project his voice so that everyone in the theatre could hear him. God used this training and George's energy and passion for the gospel to have his Word preached to many in England and America.

After George completed his studies at Oxford, he was ordained as a deacon in the Church of England. This was the usual way the church trained their ministers. After a time George would be ordained as a priest and allowed to lead his own congregation. The Church of England had strict rules on how their priests should conduct worship services. *The Book of Common Prayer* provided the liturgy and the priest was also required to use a book of printed sermons instead of writing his own. George began to run into trouble early on when he decided to preach his own sermons. Meanwhile George was off to the colony of Georgia in the New World to take over from his friend John Wesley, who had been serving the people in the struggling colony.

Music and the Gospel

Do you enjoy singing? Listening to other people sing? Music is part of our culture and, in fact, part of each human being's make up. God, our creator, gave us a capacity for music so that even if we can't play an instrument or sing well we can still enjoy listening to other people make music

Music has been used to praise God from Biblical times onward. Moses composed songs, as did Deborah, King David and Mary, the mother of Jesus. God's people have continued to use their musical talents to praise God and also to teach people what God's Word says. Whether we sing the words of scripture from the Psalms or hymns composed by Christians we are reminding ourselves of God's awesome character and his wonderful work of salvation.

Johann Sebastian Bach, born in the seventeenth century, was a gifted organist and composer. Johann loved God and among his greatest works are the *Passions*. Bach wanted people to understand what Jesus suffered at his trial and crucifixion, so he wrote a beautiful piece using the words found in the Gospel of Matthew. *The St Matthew Passion* uses two choirs, an orchestra and soloists to tell the story very clearly. It was sung in churches in Germany on Good Friday. He went on to write other cantatas about the Christmas story, the Resurrection and Jesus' Ascension. And he set Mary's 'Magnificat' found in Luke 1 to music.

Bach's music is lovely to listen to, but why would we consider it important to the church? Because Bach loved God and he wanted to teach people about him with his music. Many people still had not learned to read in the seventeenth and eighteenth century, but God's people still came faithfully to worship him every week. In church they heard God's Word read and preached, and they also heard it sung in Bach's music. Music is one more way to teach people the truths of the Bible.

That Voice

Atlantic Ocean 1738

The soldier beat the drum loudly on the deck of the *Whitaker* calling everyone on board to evening prayers. As the ship rolled gently with the waves of the Atlantic the red-coated soldiers assembled into parade formation. Sailors not on duty also gathered at the back of the company along with a few colonists bound for the Georgia Colony. They all faced the three men who stood watching them: Captain Whiting, master of the ship, Captain Mackay, the company commander, and a slight young man, George Whitefield, dressed in his black wool Genevan gown and white preaching tabs.

When all was quiet George opened the Prayer Book and began to read the evening prayers, familiar words to any who worshipped regularly in the Church of England. But instead of going on to read a sermon from the *Book of Homilies*, George began to preach. He had spent the last two months on board with these people. Many were not in the least interested in God or hearing the gospel. Even Captain Mackay, well known for his colourful language, had not made any effort to behave politely in front of George. So everyone was surprised when the captain had unexpectedly insisted that everyone attend morning and evening prayers with the ship's chaplain. George was not about to let this opportunity pass. They needed to hear about God's love for them, their need for repentance and the New Birth.

George chose the Prodigal Son as his text and, other than a few sea birds squawking overhead and the sails flapping in the breeze, there was silence as George told the story. The soldiers, who had looked bored or disgruntled, began to listen in spite of themselves.

George's voice drew them in with his vivid account of the son and his downward spiral that ended with him starving in a pig pen. The worse the boy's life became, the sadder and deeper George's voice became. Then his tone changed to one of longing as he described the father who never stopped looking for his son. The men listened and when George told them of the happy reunion some even smiled and nodded. Finally George told them they were like prodigal sons who were running away from God. They needed to turn from their wicked ways and repent, and God would receive them as that father did. Then George closed with a prayer asking the Holy Spirit to speak to each one standing on the deck.

Captain Mackay dismissed his men and shook George's hand. 'Thank you,' he said as he turned away with a thoughtful look on his face.

Captain Whiting still stood as if rooted to the deck. At last he said, 'We need to talk more of this, Mr Whitefield. Will you join me for dinner in my cabin?'

George readily agreed with a smile and a warm handshake. As the captain walked away, James Habersham approached. The young Yorkshire schoolmaster was going to take up a teaching position in the Georgia colony. 'Well done,' James said, slapping George gently on the back. 'Great sermon! You had their attention. All that time you spent getting to know the men and their families has paid off.'

George shrugged. 'God is the one who reaches into their hearts. He has just given me the gift to speak His words to them. Now, come, we must go to our cabin and pray.'

* * *

Almost two months later, twenty-four year old George stood on the deck as the ship navigated its way past the coastal islands off the Georgia colony and into the mouth of the Savannah River. George looked up at the bluffs towering above on both sides of the winding river and he grinned with the excitement of exploring this new place.

'So, what does the boy preacher think of the colony so far?' the captain asked as he joined George at the railing.

'Feels wonderfully warm after leaving a wintery England,' George commented.

'Aye, and it'll get warmer still. Summer is so humid it'll sap your energy,' the captain warned with a smile. 'But I doubt that will stop someone like you from preaching.'

'That's why I'm here. Answering God's call to preach, to the colonists and the Indians who have never heard God's Word.'

'You've practiced well on board,' the captain said. 'The sailors and soldiers who started out with us four months ago are changed men. I've watched how you've talked with my crew and the soldiers, and how you comforted any that were ill. You're not just a preacher with an amazing voice. You are a caring minister of God's Word. Thank you for leading me to Christ so I could experience the new birth.'

George smiled at his now close friend. 'Trust in the Lord. Read his Word and he will give you the strength to live for him.'

George parted from the crew and company of soldiers after many goodbyes and grateful tears. God had given George the privilege of winning almost the entire ship for him. Then, along with the colonists who were also disembarking at Savannah, George and James climbed the steep path up the bluffs to the town.

They were greeted by Charles Delmotte, the schoolmaster of Savannah that James had come to replace. He showed them around the carefully laid out town that Governor Oglethorpe had designed only five years before. The town was making good progress. Many colonists had built their wooden homes and had laid out vegetable gardens with fences to keep the cattle and goats out. But there were not as many people as George had expected, at least not as many English people. A large group of Germans had joined the colony. And there were plenty of Yamacraw Indians who had allowed Governor Oglethorpe to build Savannah on their land.

George also noticed a great many children, but they were not playing happily in the streets. They were dressed in rags and sat sadly in small groups, looking thin and undernourished.

'Who do these children belong to?' George wanted to know.

Charles Delmotte shook his head sadly. 'They are orphans. Their parents have died of disease, which is all too common here. We try to care for them, but many of the families are already struggling to feed their own children with whatever they can grow, so they don't always have enough to share. Didn't John Wesley tell you about this?'

'Yes, but I didn't think it was this bad. Something must be done. I brought some money with me but it won't be enough. At least I have the barrels of clothing from the churches. I'll see that they get those right away. But they will need much more than new clothes.'

George got busy at once. He gathered the children together and used the money he had brought to buy what food he could and gave out the clothing. Then he visited all the people in the town, looking for those who had room to take the children in for a short time. He promised them all that he would be building an orphanage to care for the orphans. There was much more he wanted to do but he needed more resources, so he went back to England to let the churches know about the need.

* * *

As George stepped onto English soil in January 1739 he had a number of things to do. First was his ordination to the priesthood, which his friend Bishop Benson was happy to do. However, the bishop did have some words of warning for George afterwards about his preaching.

'Many of the bishops are upset that you don't use the sermons printed for the prayer services. You might be wise to start using those sermons again instead of coming up with your own.'

George was puzzled. 'Those sermons are not "my own". They are straight from God's Word. What else would I preach?'

George just shook his head and continued with his plans. He would travel around the churches preaching as he had before he went to Georgia, presenting the need for the New Birth and taking up offerings for the orphanage. But it didn't turn out to be that easy.

Bishop Benson had been right. Many of the other bishops refused to let him preach in their churches. One after the other told him he wasn't welcome because his passionate sermons were not sombre enough or from the *Book of Homilies*. By the time George had arrived in Bristol to visit his sister and her husband, he was frustrated. Only a couple of churches had allowed him to preach and he had not raised enough money for the orphanage. What should he do?

Then he remembered hearing about a Welsh evangelist, Howell Harris, who was known for preaching in the fields and streets. Maybe George could do that too. While he was in Bristol he heard about the miners who lived nearby in Kingswood. Most people avoided them because they could be violent. The town had no church or anyone to preach to them, so George and his friend, William Seward, walked out one Saturday to a field near where the miners were leaving their pits for the day.

George found a small hill and stood on it. Raising his Bible in one hand, he called out to the men walking by, 'Blessed are the poor in spirit, for they shall see the kingdom of heaven.'[1]

The men stopped at the curious sight of a clergyman wearing his black robe and white periwig, and waving a Bible. Then they stayed even though they were tired and grimy from their work. As George went on preaching from the Sermon on the Mount, his voice carried across the open space to others walking by and they came over to see what was going on. Soon two hundred men and some women and children had gathered. George knew how to hold his audience. He told them about Jesus, the friend of sinners, who came to call them to righteousness. He warned about how terrible their sin was, but that God loved them so much that he

---

[1] Matthew 5:3

sent his Son to die in their place so they could have eternal life in God's Kingdom. By the end of the sermon many of those violent, bitter men had tears streaming down their coal-blacken faces, asking God to forgive them.

George was tired but triumphant that God had blessed his words that day. The next day the miners invited him back. They wanted to hear more from God's Word. George didn't hesitate. He grabbed his Bible and went out to meet a crowd of 2,000 people gathered to hear him preach. The miners provided a table for him to stand on and his powerful voice carried so that everyone could hear. They even offered to give what they could to help the orphans in the Georgia colony.

Over the next month, word spread that George Whitefield had been shut out of the Bristol churches and was preaching in an open field. People came to see and hear this new thing. Some came because they wanted to hear the gospel and others came out of curiosity. They walked, rode horses or came in carriages. By the end of the month 23,000 people were gathering. George was amazed and thankful. He asked the people to sing a psalm while he prayed that God would give him the words to speak.

God blessed George's ministry in Bristol and other parts of southern England. He didn't need church buildings to preach in, only an open field. Word would spread quickly and crowds would gather to hear him wherever he preached. By the beginning of the summer, George was ready to return to Georgia to build his orphanage and begin preaching in the colonies in North America.

* * *

George and his 'family' of volunteers, who were coming to help with the orphanage, landed in Philadelphia in October of 1739. His friend William Seward had accompanied him with a plan to purchase a sloop to help George travel up and down the American coast. So while William made his enquiries and plans, George began preaching. He stood on the steps of the courthouse in the evening preaching to a group of people that grew as time went on. People in the homes along the street opened their windows wide to hear this new preacher.

A man in his thirties left his house to see what all the fuss was about. Benjamin Franklin was a printer and inventor and was curious about anything or anyone who was new and interesting. He waited to introduce himself to George.

'That's quite a voice you have, my friend,' Benjamin said. 'And a very powerful message to go with it.'

George shook Benjamin's hand. 'Does that mean you find the call to the gospel irresistible?' he asked with an encouraging smile.

Benjamin shook his head, his shoulder-length hair swinging about his shoulders, and returned the smile. 'No, preacher, I don't, although I'm willing to hear you again. With the coming cold weather you are going to need a better place to preach than on the court steps. I'll have to see what I can do.'

'Thank you, Mr Franklin, but I'm planning to leave for New York very soon to meet a Mr Thomas Noble. He wants to help with the orphanage I'm starting in Georgia colony.'

'But, you'll be back after that, I hear from a certain Mr Seward. I'll have something organised by then,' Benjamin promised, and then invited George back to his house for a meal.

* * *

The following week George and Gilbert Tennant, a Presbyterian minister he had met in Philadelphia, rode up to New York along the muddy roads. Word that George Whitefield was coming had spread. After his meeting with Thomas Noble to receive money for the orphanage, George was invited to preach in a pasture in Manhattan, near the Hudson River. Even though it was a chilly November evening 2,000 people arrived to hear him. His strong voice rang out to the farthest ends of the crowd so that all could hear the message of Good News that he preached.

George stayed for a week, preaching often, sometimes several times a day. Then he returned to Philadelphia where Benjamin

Franklin had built him a preaching pavilion, 100 feet by 70 feet, to allow the crowds to gather out of the cold November wind. For the rest of that month, George preached almost every day. And the city of Philadelphia began to change. Benjamin, who resisted the gospel but remained good friends with George, wrote in his newspaper:

> *It was wonderful to see the Change soon made in the Manners [behaviour] of our Inhabitants; from being thoughtless or indifferent about Religion, it seem'd as if all the World were growing Religious; so that one could not walk thro' the Town in an Evening without Hearing Psalms sung in different Families of every Street.*[2]

After their stay in Philadelphia, George and William decided to send the rest of the volunteers for Georgia on the sloop William had purchased, while they rode overland. Even though George was tired, he wanted to see the other colonies and meet the people and, of course, preach wherever he was allowed.

The journey was difficult for several reasons. The land was still very sparsely populated and there were very few continuous roads from north to south in the Thirteen Colonies. So George and William had to sometimes pick their way through dense forest, fording streams and rivers or over rocky terrain. Some days they made very slow progress. As nightfall approached, they would hope to find an inn, but if not, then they relied on the kindness of strangers to allow them a bed for a night in their remote homes.

When they came to major towns, they were often greeted with suspicion by the clergy in the churches. George's reputation as a preacher had preceded him and while the people wanted to hear him preach, the ministers didn't want him in their churches. George was critical of ministers who failed to preach the gospel

---

[2] *Benjamin Franklin on Rev. George Whitefield, 1739.* National Humanities Center. http://nationalhumanitiescenter.org/pds/becomingamer/ideas/text2/franklinwhitefield.pdf (accessed March 2013).

clearly, which angered them. They also didn't approve of his sermons because they didn't come from prepared texts.

Lastly, George was troubled as they moved further south and passed plantations that had huge slave populations working their fields. He was angry when he saw the way overseers whipped the workers and was disgusted with their poor housing conditions. So George and William began to stop at the plantations, visiting the slaves after their work was done and preaching the hope of the gospel to them. Then George would tell the plantation owners to treat their slaves with kindness as Paul urged masters to do in the Bible.[3]

When George and William arrived in Charlestown, the only way to safely get to Savannah was by canoe along the coast. So they hired a canoe complete with some strong black slaves to row it late in January 1740. George was exhausted from the journey and his heavy preaching schedule. He found he couldn't eat and his nerves caused him to jump at every noise, but the journey in the canoe allowed him a short time to rest quietly.

When the men arrived in Savannah, they were greeted by James Habersham and the group of volunteers, all eager to get started on the orphanage. When George looked at their eager faces he felt guilty for saying he needed to rest a few days first. But James Habersham understood.

'Get some rest, George. I already have the plot of land cleared and fenced while we waited for you. When you are recovered we can all discuss the plans for the buildings.'

George fully intended to rest but the next day he was sitting out on the porch of James's house when he saw three German orphans dressed in dirty rags. They were sitting near the fence of James's property. Full of concern, George walked over to them.

'Are you boys hungry?' he asked. When they didn't seem to understand his question, he motioned with his hands to show eating a bowl of soup.

---

[3] Colossians 4:1

The boys nodded vigorously and started to rise. But one couldn't get up because he was so weak and miserable. George bent down and picked him up and motioned for the others to follow him into the house. There George supervised their meal and then found some warm clothes for them. Lastly, he showed them his bed and encouraged all three to climb in. They fell asleep instantly. Leaving them to their rest, George walked out of the house to look for William and James. There was no time to rest. Orphans were starving. They needed the orphanage now.

George and William consulted about the plans and decided that they would think big. Several buildings were to be erected on the property ten miles north of the town. They hired thirty workers, bricklayers, carpenters and sawyers to complete the orphanage as soon as possible. Then he arranged to use a vacant building as a temporary home for the orphans, gathering them together under one roof and organising his 'family' of volunteers to care for them.

Meanwhile, even though he still wasn't feeling well, George preached in Savannah on Sunday, holding five services that day all focused on justification by faith. Then he took a short trip south to see Governor Oglethorpe and tell him about the progress of the orphanage.

When George returned to Savannah he divided his time between supervising the building project, preaching every Sunday and collecting food to feed the poor of the town. Not surprisingly, George's health didn't improve, but he refused to slow down.

In March the orphanage opened. George led a service of thanksgiving outside the main two storey building that would house the children. Two smaller buildings, the infirmary and the workhouse where the children would be trained in trades stood behind the main building.

'I have decided to name this place Bethesda, or House of Mercy,' George announced. 'May it be used to show mercy and care for those who cannot care for themselves.'

The Great Awakening
18th Century (or the 1700s)

George was only twenty-five years old when the orphanage was completed. He still had much more work to do in the American colonies. Although his health was never very good he didn't slow down. Instead he continued his preaching tours up and down the Thirteen Colonies. He also took time to return to Britain to preach in England, Scotland, Wales and Ireland. When people told him to take time to rest, he responded by saying, 'I'd rather wear out than rust out.' And he did wear himself out serving God. He died at the age of fifty-six from heart failure.

God used George Whitefield in a mighty way. His preaching in America began an awakening of interest in the gospel that had not been there before. There were, of course, Christians in the colonies and faithful ministers too. But many other people who had come to settle in the colonies from England and Europe came because they thought they could do as they pleased in a new land. They weren't interested in hearing the gospel. That is, until God sent a gifted young man with a powerful voice to preach to them.

Jonathan Edwards, a New England minister, was also part of the Great Awakening. He preached faithfully each week to his congregation in Massachusetts. His printed sermons stirred many people to faith who could not hear him preach in person.

Back in England, an awakening was also taking place. John Wesley and his brother Charles were preaching in churches and out of doors in order to reach as many people as possible with the Good News of the Gospel. Historians say that Wesley's preaching changed

British society. The people had been indifferent to God's Word and the society was lax with its laws and morals. But God's Word changed that. People were converted in large numbers and began to obey God's Word, thereby changing attitudes in the society. What an exciting time it must have been in both Britain and the New World.

Twenty-seven years after George Whitefield died, Mary Lyon was born on a farm in Massachusetts in 1797. By the time Mary was grown up she had done something few young women her age did: she went to school. Not just a small one room school to learn to read and write, but she also attended a new type of school called a female academy. Previously only boys were allowed to receive a higher education, but times were slowly changing. Mary had a huge thirst for knowledge. When a new female academy closed after a short time due to lack of money, she would go to the next school or find a professor who was willing to teach a young woman. In the early 1800's Mary was considered a bit strange for wanting all that education, but God had placed this thirst inside her for a reason. He had a job for Mary to do and he gave her the gifts to do it.

Mary was converted at the age of nineteen, and she pursued her spiritual studies in God's Word with as much enthusiasm as she studied chemistry and physics. Mary became a mature Christian with a broad education, and she was full of energy and enthusiasm to serve God and to teach other women what she had learned. So the obvious thing to do was to start a seminary or a college for women.

Accomplishing a Great Work
Ipswich, Massachusetts 1834

Mary pushed her red hair into her white brimmed cap before her small bedroom mirror. Then she shook her head and the hair came tumbling out. Mary sighed and started again, this time going slower and with more care. She could almost hear Amanda, her former school friend, laughing at her. Amanda had been like a sister to Mary when they had boarded with the White family while attending Sanderson Academy. Amanda, always lovely and well dressed, had tried her best to give Mary advice on her clothing and hair. Mary appreciated the advice, but had to admit that she didn't give her appearance much thought, beyond tidiness and cleanliness.

What really occupied thirty-five-year-old Mary's mind was learning as much as she could and teaching others. God had been good to her. Each time she thought the door to higher education had been closed to her, another opportunity would present itself and Mary was able once more to study. Now she wanted to provide those same opportunities to other young women, only in a permanent place so they could complete their education.

Mary walked down the corridor of the Ipswich Female Seminary, her heeled shoes sounding on the wooden floors with every step. She passed several classrooms where teachers were preparing for the autumn semester, and arrived at the principal's office. She knocked and opened the door at the invitation from within.

Zilpah Grant, the principal, turned in her chair away from her paper-littered desk and smiled at Mary. Zilpah, although still pretty at age forty, was very pale and fragile looking after her long illness. A stab of guilt went through Mary as she took a chair near the window. Should she really leave her teaching position at Ipswich Seminary with Zilpah still not quite recovered?

'So, tell me, how did your meeting go yesterday?' Zilpah asked, laying down her pen and folding her hands in her lap. She sat still, ready to listen.

'Wonderful!' Mary replied with a wide smile. 'Professor Hitchcock has assembled a group of devout Christian ministers and laymen to form a board of trustees for the new seminary. They were excited about raising the funds and choosing a location. Rev. Hawks is especially keen and has promised to take a leave from his church to be a full-time fundraiser. My school is looking more and more like a reality!'

As Mary continued to tell Zilpah of the details she spoke with her whole body, moving her hands in time with the flow of her words and shifting this way and that in her chair with her enthusiasm. Then she suddenly slowed down and said, 'But I feel guilty leaving you like this.'

'Nonsense,' Zilpah replied. 'You and I have prayed about this for over a year. God has shown you the way to move forward and you would be wrong to give up now. We both know that I will have to retire soon. I'm unlikely to be much stronger and the funding for this school is running out. Young women blessed with a thirst for learning and desire to serve God need your new school.'

Mary left her chair and hugged her friend and co-worker. 'Bless you. I'm so thankful for your unselfish friendship.'

Zilpah pushed her away gently. 'So, go now and do as God has bid you. I will continue to pray and write you encouraging letters.'

Mary straightened up. 'And I will answer every one of them,' she promised.

After Mary said her farewells to the other teachers and some of the early arriving students, she packed her trunk with her few clothes and many books and left the town of Ipswich. Travelling by coach over the bumpy roads of Massachusetts, Mary arrived in the town of Amherst to board with Professor Hitchcock and his family while the plans for the new seminary were being carried out.

Over the next year, Mary travelled throughout the towns and villages in eastern Massachusetts, visiting churches and women's groups, telling them about the new seminary and asking that they consider giving what they could to the new enterprise. She returned each time to the Hitchcock home where she shared stories of those meetings and how well the new seminary was received.

'Many people, especially women, were pleased to hear what I had to say,' Mary told them as they sat in the cosy Hitchcock front room. A fire burned cheerfully in the stone fireplace they sat around. Mary and Mrs Hitchcock sat in high-backed wooden chairs while Professor Hitchcock enjoyed his new padded wing chair that was a gift from his wife.

'All of them?' Orra Hitchcock asked with raised eyebrows. 'One newspaper I read has called you a "masculine woman" because you want to educate women. Not very kind.'

Mary shook her head with a rueful smile. 'Oh yes, there were some who objected. One deacon, who had come had been dragged along by his wife, spoke up quite sharply.'

Orra's eyes sparkled with mischief. 'And did you put him in his place?'

'Orra, please,' her husband interrupted. 'That's not a very Christian attitude. I'm sure Mary was respectful of the poor man.'

Mary laughed at their banter. 'Yes, I did my best to be winsome, even though he irritated me. I pointed out that women who planned to marry need a good education because they are their children's first teachers. Not only do they teach their children the ABCs but they also teach them about God and his Word. So, of course, they would need proper instruction themselves. And then for those women who don't marry, a good education trains them to be teachers and missionaries. The poor man had difficulty grasping the ideas, but his wife was nodding vigorously.'

'More importantly, did anyone pledge any money to the seminary?' Professor Hitchcock asked.

'Very practical question, sir,' Mary replied. 'I collected $120 in cash and pledges. It doesn't match the generous gift of $1,200 the ladies at Ipswich sent me, but it will help nonetheless. We are well on our way to establishing the endowment for the new seminary.'

'Well done, my dear,' Orra said. 'Now I think there is time for you to have a rest before dinner is served. You look tired. The maid and I prepared your room for you this morning.'

Mary's eyes filled with happy tears. 'Thank you. God has given me such a great gift in your friendship. I'm so happy to be able to call your home mine, too.' She gave them both a hug and headed up the staircase to her room. Then she stopped and turned back. 'What about your children? Is all well with them?'

Orra nodded. 'As rambunctious as usual, but working on the Latin conjugations that you assigned them. They will recite them for you after dinner.'

Mary smiled. 'I'll look forward to that.'

Mary spent her 'resting' time over the next few weeks writing letters to family, friends and those who had pledged their support. She also continued teaching the Hitchcock children and pursuing her own studies just for the joy of it. Then she began travelling again, this time visiting towns and villages in western Massachusetts. She met many people on the coaches. With her winning ways she made them her friends and encouraged them to support her new school as the horses climbed the gentle hills and descended into the green valleys.

There continued to be objections to the new seminary. Some criticised Mary's plan to keep the tuition fees as low as possible by asking the students to do chores at the school. This new idea was viewed with suspicion, but Mary insisted that all young women, whether rich or poor, should have an opportunity to attend her school and this was the way to make it possible. She also planned to pay her teachers less and they, too, would help with the chores. Again, Mary was criticised for not planning to pay proper wages. Mary carried on with her fundraising, ignoring her critics as much as possible.

By 1836 the Trustees had chosen the town of South Hadley for the new seminary, and the name Mount Holyoke, after the name of a nearby mountain. The Mount Holyoke Female Seminary was issued with its charter by the state of Massachusetts and the building began. One year later, the seminary was on its way to being completed. Mary began to hire teachers who willingly supported her plans and then began advertising for students to apply for the first classes beginning in November. The mail began to pour in.

Mary sat at her desk in the bedroom of Mr and Mrs Condit's home. They lived next to the Seminary and had invited Mary to stay with them during the final months of building. Her desk was covered with over 200 letters from women who wanted to come to Mount Holyoke. Mary had not imagined that there would be so many. And she knew that the school only had room for eighty women. *I'll have to begin planning a new wing to the school already,* she thought with a happy smile. Then she began to open the letters, sorting them into piles of hopefuls, probables and probably nots. She then met with her teachers and together they decided who the best candidates were for the first year. It was a long task, but Mary couldn't be happier.

The doors of the seminary opened on November 8, 1837 even though the building wasn't quite ready. While Mary stood at the door, whose front step was still missing, awaiting the arrival of her students, others were busy around her. Painters were finishing up in the double parlours. Deacon Safford was on his knees tacking down matting in the upstairs hall. In the basement kitchen, Mrs Safford and Mrs Porter were washing up crockery and preparing a light meal for the students, while some local women were stitching comforters. Workmen were busy installing the Rumford oven and someone else was measuring the windows for blinds. Outside, wagons were pulling up with furniture that had been delayed by storms, followed by some of the village men who had come to help move it into the seminary. Behind them were carriages and coaches with young women arriving for their first day of higher education.

Mary welcomed them all with a smile and an enthusiastic handshake. The bustle around her only added to her pleasure and excitement. 'Welcome, welcome to our hive of activity,' she greeted each student. 'Please go through to the teaching hall on your right and find a chair, if there are any there yet,' she said with a small laugh. 'Isn't it all wonderful!'

When a good number of women had arrived, Mary went to speak to them in the hall with her three teachers standing behind her. As she looked out over the students she saw quite a variety. Some were as young as sixteen while others were in their mid-twenties. Some were obviously from farming communities with their home-spun cotton dresses and plain bonnets, while others were more expensively dressed. This was exactly what Mary had hoped for; a student body based on intellectual ability and not on wealth.

'I'm so glad you are all here,' she began. 'This will be your home and your school, so let me tell you what is where. On this floor is the teaching hall, which you are standing in. There is also a reading room and library, two double parlours and my lodging rooms. The top three floors are scholars' and teachers' lodgings, sixteen in each storey. You will be shown to your room shortly. In the basement is our kitchen, pantry and dining room. Your tuition is partly covered by your domestic chores. So we will be our own cooks and cleaners as well as students and teachers. I have drawn up a schedule so that all the tasks are divided evenly. There should be no complaints because not only are you working for your tuition but you are also serving your classmates and teachers. You should do so with a cheerful countenance because we are all serving God. Now, you will notice we are a little short of beds and linens. There have been some delays in the deliveries … ah, here are some of them now.' Mary beckoned some village men who were cautiously looking in the doorway. 'Do bring in the furniture. Deacon Safford is just up those stairs and he will show you where they go.'

Even as the men came and went with bedsteads, chairs and desks, Mary continued her speech. 'As you see, all will be well, if a little chaotic at first,' she began again with an engaging smile. 'But we are resourceful and I'm sure it will work out just fine. Now on to your entrance examinations. They will be oral exams over the next few days. I'm confident you will all pass, but these exams will give me a better idea at what level to place you. Now, ladies, let us commit the first year of Mount Holyoke Female Seminary to our Lord.'

Everyone bowed their heads as Mary offered a short prayer of thanksgiving to God for this new venture. Then she nodded to her teachers to begin by sorting out which student went to which room. The women dispersed with much chattering and began to explore their new home. Mary's enthusiasm was catching and instead of being dismayed by all the noise and activity, the young women happily rolled up their sleeves and began to help out with making up beds and moving small pieces of furniture with the local lads.

'I don't see how we can begin with all this chaos,' Miss Peters muttered.

Mary laughed. 'All will be well, you will see. Anything new takes time to organise. And we all have to help. Why don't you go and see how the men installing the new Rumford oven in the basement are getting on. And don't worry.'

Mary patted Miss Peters' shoulder as she turned away. Mary wondered if Miss Peters was really up to this new way of doing things. She had come highly recommended by her previous school for her teaching ability. Time would tell if she could adapt to the Mount Holyoke way of doing things.

Mary spent the next week meeting with each young woman and giving the oral exams in English, Mathematics, History, Chemistry, Physics and Biblical Knowledge. Mary had to hunt down the students because each was busy helping out wherever they were needed. Sometimes the exams took place in the kitchen while Mary helped a student dry the dishes. Sometimes she found her quarry sorting linens so they sat on the bed while Mary asked the questions. In between exams, Mary went to help each of the groups of women at their chores, getting to know each young woman a little better. This meant that Mary woke up at 4 a.m. every day to help in the kitchen to get the breakfast ready. She made the dough for the bread and set it to rise by the warm fireplace. While she waited, she set up her portable writing desk and wrote letters until 5 a.m. when the breakfast students arrived. They set the five long tables, baked the bread, peeled and boiled the potatoes and filled the water kettles to heat the water for washing up. After breakfast was cleared and cleaned up, the morning classes began.

Each morning began with devotions and was then divided between domestic chores and classroom studies. In the evenings, Mary invited a few students at a time to her office, where she spent time studying the Bible with them and urging each one to examine their hearts to see if they belonged to God. By the following March, Mary had met with each of her students and was pleased to see that many had made professions of faith. The seminary was running well, except for Miss Peters, who finally burst into tears one day in Mary's office. She couldn't stay any longer. She was not used to teaching in this kind of institution and she wouldn't stay. Mary had nodded sadly and wished her well.

Over all, Mary was very happy with the first year of students. She wrote a circular letter to all those who had and were supporting the seminary with their money and their prayers. She reported on the good progress, ending the letter with: 'It is like fitting out our first little band of missionaries.'

Inventions and the Gospel

19th Century (or the 1800s)

Mary Lyon was responsible for educating and sending out a number of missionaries over the next ten years. Fidelia Fiske went to Persia, now Iran, to start a school for girls. Susan Tolman married Cyrus Mills and they went to Ceylon, now Sri Lanka, as missionaries. Ellen Whitmore and Sarah Worcester travelled 3,000 miles across the U.S.A. to become teachers at the first Cherokee National Female Seminary. Then, two years later, Ellen married missionary Warren Goodale and went to Hawaii to serve. Abby Allen Fairbank went to India, as did Harriet Newell. Charlotte Grout accompanied her husband as a missionary to south-east Africa. The list went on and on. Mary Lyon taught all of these women and, in turn, they went around the world to share the gospel with others. Even after Mary died in 1849, her teaching still had an impact on the world through her students.

Beginning in the late eighteenth century and on through the nineteenth century, Christians began to form missionary societies to send out missionaries around the world. The Great Awakening had begun a new era in the church. The emphasis on personal conversion and concern to grow spiritually through daily Bible reading and prayer had revitalised Christians in Europe and America. They wanted to share the wonder and power of the gospel with everyone. With new inventions like the steam engine, first by Thomas Savery and then James Watts, travel became faster. Ships didn't have to rely on the wind to move them across the oceans, and on land trains could travel faster than horse and coach. Now it was much easier to head out to foreign countries or remote regions of a continent.

Along with these inventions came the idea that science had many answers that would make life better for people. And indeed, many of the inventions during the nineteenth century did just that. Early in the century gas and then electric lighting was invented. How much nicer it was to have modern lighting rather than to have to carry a candle around your house in the evenings. Small machines like typewriters, sewing machines, washing machines and eventually vacuum cleaners made work in offices and the home much easier. Communication was improved with, first, the invention of the telegraph and then the telephone. And people could get around more easily on early bicycles and eventually early cars, if they were wealthy enough to afford one. Louis Pasteur discovered the causes of many diseases which led to improvements in medicine. He also discovered the existence of viruses, which led to more research and understanding of diseases. As the century wore on, people began to think that if science could do all that, then maybe all they had to do was keep studying and inventing and eventually life would be so improved there would be no more sickness or sadness, no need for wars and no need for God. Of course, that isn't what happened.

No invention, however beneficial to people, can take away the root of the problem: our sin. We were originally created to serve God with joy, but we can't because our sinful condition has created a huge barrier between us and God, who is perfect. But as we know, God didn't abandon his fallen creation. Instead he sent his Son to live a perfect life on earth and then to die in our place. Jesus then defeated death and came back to life. Only through his sacrifice can we be forgiven and our sin wiped out. That was the message, the gospel, which people were forgetting amid all their useful inventions. So preachers were needed, as always, to keep preaching the Good News.

In most places in the west, there were those who benefitted from all the changes in how people lived and worked, and there were also those who did not. Many working people's lives became harder with the inventions of machines because their employers expected them to work longer and faster than ever before. If they couldn't keep up with the changes then they lost their jobs. Or worse yet, their jobs disappeared when a machine could do it faster. So along with the wealth and ease that many people lived with, many others' lives became poorer and more difficult. Society was not changing for the better for everyone.

In 1834, when Mary Lyon was making her plans for Holyoke Seminary, Charles Spurgeon was born into a family of preachers in England. Charles spent much of his early life in his grandparents' manse in Stambourne because his mother was too ill to care for him. Charles heard God's Word preached and discussed from the time he could understand. He loved to read and often lost himself in his grandfather's library of theology books. Charles was converted when he was sixteen and he joined the Baptist church. Almost immediately, the pastor recognised that Charles had the gift of preaching. First, Charles taught Sunday school and then a year later he was encouraged to accept a call to a small church in Waterbeach, just outside Cambridge. The following year, when Charles was only eighteen, he accepted a call to New Park Street Baptist Church in London. The boy preacher from the countryside caused quite a stir in the big city. Right from the beginning, Charles received both praise and criticism for his preaching. Some said his speech was too theatrical and his dress sense was all wrong. But others heard the gospel with such a strong understanding that they responded and were converted. And New Park Street Church began to grow until there wasn't enough room for all those who wanted to hear God's Word preached. And there was one young woman, Susannah Thompson, who eventually thought the young preacher worthy and accepted his proposal to marry him.

The Prince of Preachers
London 1856

'Welcome to our new home, Susie,' Charles said as he opened the door of their four-storey terraced house. He gave Susannah, his heavily pregnant wife, his arm and led her inside. Mrs Thompson, Susannah's mother, followed, her arms full of blankets. Both ladies' long, wide skirts rustled as they walked.

Susannah smiled at her enthusiastic husband and then winced. 'I'd better sit down,' she said. 'It was a bumpy ride and I think the little one inside is feeling rather upset.'

'Of course,' Charles replied, looking around the empty room. Then he spied a wooden Windsor chair in the corner and moved quickly to bring it to her. 'Are you comfortable? Is there something you need?'

Susannah shook her head, making her ringlets dance across her face. 'I'll be fine here. You show the removal men where to put the rest of our furniture.' Then she turned to her mother. 'Once the bed is set up, Mama, I think I should lie down.'

Mrs Thompson nodded as she headed toward the staircase. 'I'll put these in the bedroom, ready to make up the bed when it arrives.'

Meanwhile, with a worried backward glance on his broad face, Charles went to the front door to call in the men with the furniture. A few hours later Susannah was comfortably propped up in bed while her mother unpacked a trunk full of linens. Charles arrived to inform them both that the men had gone and he had put the kettle on to boil for tea.

'Is your time near, my dear?' he asked. 'Should I fetch the midwife?'

Susannah patted his hand. 'Not yet, but very soon. Don't worry so much. Now tell me all about the plans for the music hall,' she said, with some mischief in her eyes.

Mrs Thompson shook her head, but said with a smile, 'Who would have thought I'd be worshipping in such a place as Surrey Gardens Music Hall!'

Twenty-two-year-old Charles laughed and, feeling a little better about his wife's condition, sat down on an upholstered chair beside the bed. 'Praise God that such a place can be used for such a worthy purpose. I'm very grateful that the deacons agreed to let us meet there. The New Park Street Chapel is just too small to accommodate the morning congregation.'

'Well, that's because everyone wants to hear the great preacher,' Susannah replied. 'How many will the music hall hold?'

'About 10,000, but I'm sure it won't be filled.'

'Meanwhile, what about the plans to build a new church building?' Mrs Thompson asked as she finished her task and sat down on the closed lid of the trunk. 'I can't see meeting in the music hall indefinitely.'

Charles nodded. 'We will need to do a lot of fundraising first, so we can afford it. The deacons have appointed a committee to make the plans. Now I imagine we could all use some tea.'

Mrs Thompson rose quickly. 'I'll see to it. You stay with Susannah.'

* * *

Ten days later Susannah gave birth to not one, but two, baby boys. She looked very tired and weak when Charles was at last allowed to come into the bedroom. He rushed over to the bed and kissed her forehead. He would have hugged her, but she looked too fragile and he was afraid he would hurt her.

'Will she be alright?' he asked the midwife anxiously.

'It was a difficult birth, and she is very tired. But all is well,' the brisk woman assured him. 'Would you like to see your sons?'

Mrs Thompson, who had helped during the labour, brought a tightly wrapped baby and put him in Charles' arms. Then she picked up a similar looking bundle from the small cradle by the bed. 'Aren't they beautiful?' she whispered.

Charles looked down at the sleeping baby and then peered over at his twin. 'Wonderful,' he breathed. 'True gifts from God.'

'I'd like to name them Charles and Thomas,' Susannah's weak voice sounded from the bed.

Charles carried his namesake over to the bed and placed the baby beside her. 'Those are excellent choices, wifey. You, too, are a great gift from God. Thank you for such wonderful sons.'

'Now she needs to rest,' Mrs Thompson said firmly and shooed Charles out of the room.

Charles felt like he was on top of the world and praised God for all his blessings. God had taken a country boy, brought him to the big city and made him a great preacher before Charles was even twenty-five years old. Then he had given Charles a loving wife and two strong baby boys. Now God was blessing Charles' ministry and growing his congregation right out of their church building. God was indeed good.

One month later, Charles kissed Susannah goodbye, as she lay in her bed still recovering, with his two sons nearby in their cradles, and left for the Surrey Gardens Music Hall. As his carriage pulled up to the enormous building he was amazed to see the people standing outside. Swallowing hard to calm himself, he stepped down from the carriage and walked around to the side entrance. He had not expected to fill the hall on the first night. Once inside, he met with the deacons for a time of prayer before stepping out onto the stage.

Charles took a seat and looked out over the music hall, while the music director led the congregation in singing several hymns. People had filled every seat on the main floor as well as in the two levels of galleries that lined the walls under the enormous glass-domed ceiling. They were even sitting on the stairs and on the floor of the aisles. His heart began to beat very fast. How would they all hear him? Did he really have the right to be preaching to so many? Then he began to look more closely at the people. He saw familiar faces from his congregation seated among many strangers. Some were well dressed and sitting comfortably. Others were poorly dressed and looked strained and underfed. All at once Charles knew they all needed to hear the gospel, rich or poor, church-goer or not. So he stood up and moved forward to the podium. He began with prayer, asking for God's blessing.

Suddenly someone in the top gallery cried out, 'Fire! Fire!'

Charles stopped praying and people began to look around with concern.

Then a voice from the ground floor called out, 'The galleries are falling!' And a third voice shouted, 'The whole building is collapsing!'

Everyone began to panic. People on the ground floor rushed from their seats for the doors. People in the galleries began to run to the stairwells that were already full of people.

Charles called out in as loud a voice as he could for people to remain calm and leave in an orderly fashion, but the noise was too great and no one heard him. Then, to his horror, Charles watched the crowd on the second gallery press so hard on the railing that it gave way and several people fell to the ground floor, followed by a few more that jumped rather than be crushed in the crowd. Screams of fear and pain sounded throughout the hall as people pushed and pulled others trying to get out of the building.

'Stop! Stop!' Charles called out in vain, now almost in tears as he witnessed the terrible panic. There was nothing he could do but watch in horror.

Then Charles felt hands on his arms pulling him off the stage and into the little room where he had so recently prayed with his deacons. Tears flowed down his cheeks and he was shaking.

'Get him a chair,' someone called. 'He is near to fainting.'

The last thing Charles remembered was falling toward the floor.

A few minutes later, Charles revived enough to walk with help to the waiting carriage by the side entrance. Wrapped in blankets to keep his teeth from chattering with cold and shock, his friend Joseph Passmore and a couple of deacons rushed him to his home, where he stumbled in the door and sank into a large chair in the front room.

Susannah heard the clatter and left her bed to see what was going on. Wrapped in several shawls, she crept down the staircase in time to hear her mother announce that she would make some strong sweet tea for him. When she peered through the doorway and saw Charles, white-faced and shivering, she set aside her modesty and rushed to his side. Kneeling by the chair she took his cold hand in hers and spoke softly to him. But he did not respond.

'What happened to him?' Susannah demanded.

Briefly one of the deacons told her about the events at the music hall.

'He needs quiet and rest,' Mrs Thompson said as she came back into the room. 'And he'll not get it here, with two small babies and a wife that should be in bed.' She looked sternly at her daughter.

Susannah reluctantly nodded. 'And everyone in the congregation is likely to call, too. He'll have no peace at all.' As she stood up a sudden wave of weakness came over her and Mrs Thompson rushed over to catch her.

'To bed with you, my girl. Gentlemen, you need to find a place for Charles to recuperate. His nerves are badly shaken,' Mrs Thompson said as she led Susannah back to the staircase.

After much discussion, the men decided to take Charles to a friend's home just outside of London and not tell anyone other than his wife where he was.

Charles only vaguely heard the discussion. He couldn't talk or move much on his own, even though he had wanted to reassure his wife. He allowed the men to lift him out of the chair, wrap him in the blankets once more and lead him back out to the horse-drawn carriage on the street.

When he woke the next morning he remembered nothing of the journey or arriving at the home. He lay awake but with no energy to get out of the bed or show any interest in his hosts. He stared at the ceiling and wept while the scenes of panic and death replayed in his mind. How could this have happened? God had been blessing his ministry. Yes, there had been reports in the newspapers criticising his style of preaching, but that hadn't stopped people from coming to hear the gospel preached. Had he been too arrogant, wanting to preach to so many people all at once? Did God want him to stop preaching and let someone else take over? What about the families of the dead and injured? Why did they have to suffer? On and on the questions tumbled in his mind as he began to toss and turn in his bed.

After several days of misery and lethargy, Charles finally pushed back the covers and got up. He found he was weak from refusing to eat and took his time dressing. Emerging from his room, the wife of his host immediately offered him some tea and toast, which he accepted gratefully. Afterwards, he went out into the garden intending to stroll, but found a chair instead. He sat for a while, not really seeing the last of the autumn blooms or hearing the birds chirping.

This set a pattern that he kept to each day, until he had finally built up his strength and began strolling along the garden paths. Once more the questions and pain surfaced until he thought he could bear it no longer. Suddenly a Bible verse about Jesus Christ came into his mind.

> *Therefore God has highly exalted him and bestowed on him the name that is above every name.*[1]

It was Jesus' name that mattered, not Charles Spurgeon. God has already exalted Jesus' name higher than any other through his death and resurrection. No one on earth could change that. So even if people blamed Charles for the tragedy, God knew the truth. God

---

[1] Philippians 2:9

had commissioned him to preach the gospel, and with God's help, that's what he would do.

The next day Charles packed up his few belongings, thanked his hosts for their patience and hospitality and took a horse-drawn cab back to his home in London. Susannah, now up from her bed and feeling better, ran to hug and kiss him.

'Come sit by the fire, Charles. You look so thin and worn out. Haven't you been eating?'

Charles followed her to the settee and sat down with Susannah and put his arm around her. 'I've had no interest in food all week, but I'm doing better now. God has been speaking to me through his Word and teaching me and I'm beginning to feel stronger.'

'Then I shall see to the dinner.' Susannah moved out of the embrace, but Charles tightened his grip on her.

'Wait. I want your help this afternoon. I need to prepare my sermons for Sunday and I'd like you to read to me some of the commentaries. My head still hurts a little and I'd value your company and encouragement.'

'Of course,' Susannah agreed with a smile. But then she frowned. 'Are you sure you should go back into the pulpit so soon? There's been ...' and she hesitated. Charles waited with some concern. Finally she finished in a rush, 'a lot of criticism of you and the church in the papers. Nasty accusations. It's been quite horrible.'

Charles held her close to him. 'I'm sorry you had to see all those things printed in the papers and that I wasn't here with you. But I want to you remember that my name doesn't matter. Only Jesus' name, whom God has exalted above all names, matters. If God wants me to sacrifice my reputation for his sake, then I will do it. He will give us both the strength that we need.'

Susannah returned his hug with surprising strength. 'Then you can count on me to always be at your side. I'll set the dinner cooking and meet you in your study shortly.'

The next day his friend Joseph Passmore came to visit. He settled his lean body into an upholstered chair opposite Charles and stroked his dark beard as he studied his friend.

'You've had a nasty shock,' Joseph stated. 'Has anyone told you about that night?'

Charles shook his head, his hands twisting around each other. His nerves were still not entirely at ease. 'Susannah has told me a little, but is afraid to tell me too much. I feel so badly that she had to bear all this on her own.'

'You have a strong wife,' Joseph assured him. 'Let me tell you the statistics. Seven people died and twenty-eight were wounded, some seriously. They were all taken to hospital. No one knows what actually happened. There was no fire and no danger of collapse. If it was a prank, it was a deadly one. And certainly not your fault.'

Charles bowed his head as if someone had piled a heavy weight on his shoulders. Then taking a deep breath he said, 'I must visit all those families, of both the dead and the wounded. I'll also ask the deacons to start a fund to help those families with any needs they might have.'

Joseph agreed. 'I'll start the fund with £100 to encourage others to give. Now I hope you will be preaching this Sunday? The congregation needs to see and hear you. They, too, were discouraged by the catastrophe and they need their pastor.'

'Thank you, my friend, for both your money and your encouragement.'

That Sunday, Charles preached in New Park Street Chapel, much to the joy of his congregation. True to his word, over the next few weeks, he visited the victims in hospital and their families at home with the promise of the money to help with their medical bills. They all received him graciously, for which Charles was grateful. The newspapers continued to sneer at Charles, but he ignored them, asking God to give him the grace to continue preaching.

As a result of the tragedy, the building committee got to work immediately. They hired an architect to design a new church building.

Then Charles began to preach in London and around Britain to raise the money necessary to build it. It took five years to complete the building and, on March 31, 1861, the first service was held in the new Metropolitan Tabernacle. The 3,600 seat church was filled every Sunday, morning and evening, as well as on Thursdays.

During the years following, not only did Charles preach whenever he was invited to, but he also cared for his congregation, wrote books, established an orphanage for boys and continued to teach at his Pastors' College. The college had been started in 1857 when a number of young men came to Charles to ask for instruction in preaching. Since that time, Charles added lecturing to his students as part of his weekly duties. As time went on he decided to have the lectures published, so he showed them to Susannah for her opinion.

They were sitting in Charles' study one afternoon. Charles was at his desk, Susannah was in a chair by the window with her portable writing desk on her lap. She was reading over the manuscript, stopping to write a comment or correction in the margins. When she had finished, she tidied up the bundle of papers.

'They are excellent, Charles. Not only should you publish these, but I think every minister in England should have a copy.'

Charles looked up from his work and smiled. 'Well, my dear. If you think that why don't you do something about it? How much money will you give to purchase the books?'

Susannah looked thoughtfully at him and smiled. 'I have a little money that Father gave me. How much would 100 books cost?'

Charles grinned and set down his pen. 'I don't know, but Joseph will be able to tell us. And, what about advertising it in the next issue of *The Sword and the Trowel*?[2] We could tell all those ministers who wanted a copy to write and ask for one. This could be your project.'

Susannah nodded, her enthusiasm building. 'Could we also start a Book Fund that would help distribute other material that would

---

[2] *The Sword and the Trowel*: a monthly magazine edited by Charles Spurgeon. It began publication in 1865.

be helpful to pastors? Could that be advertised in the magazine too?'

Charles agreed and, setting aside the sermon he had been working on, he began a letter to his publisher and friend Joseph Passmore telling him of Susannah's plan.

Chocolates and the Gospel:
What is in your pocket?

Helen Cadbury was born in England and was the daughter of the president of Cadbury Chocolates. In 1893, Helen was converted at twelve years old. She was so excited about her faith that she shared it with girlfriends and they, too, became Christians. Next she formed a club with her friends called *The Pocket New Testament League*. They sewed pockets into their dresses just the right size to carry a pocket New Testament. They also carried a pledge card that they had signed. It was a promise to read their Bible every day, pray, and share their faith.

Helen and her friends kept their pledge to Read, Carry and Share as they grew up. One day Helen met gospel singer Charles Alexander and they later married. Charles travelled with evangelist D. L. Moody and sang at his meetings. Helen accompanied him, and the idea to expand the New Testament League happened on these trips. In 1908 Helen and Charles began to distribute free New Testaments as they travelled from city to city and country to country. More Christians became interested in the League and joined. Over the years the League has grown to be international and has distributed New Testaments to soldiers in the World Wars, as well as other wars and skirmishes during the last century.

Helen Cadbury Alexander died in 1969 but the Pocket New Testament League continues even today. Over 110 million New Testaments have been distributed since the League began. All it took was for one twelve-year-old girl who wanted to wield the Sword of God's Word. She said, 'If only we could get people to read the Book for themselves it will surely lead them to Christ.'

Moving into the 20th Century

Charles continued to preach and teach for fifteen more years. In that time he also continued to write and publish his sermons, devotional material and commentaries. He spoke out against the theory of evolution when it was first introduced by Charles Darwin in 1859. He also took on ministers who began to listen to German liberal theologians who taught that not everything in the Bible was true. This made Charles unpopular, but he was doing his duty as God's preacher, warning the church against heresies. Charles died in 1892 at the age of fifty-eight. Many ministers were trained under Charles Spurgeon so that the Word of God continued to be preached.

The pace of the world continued to increase as the nineteenth century came to an end and the twentieth began. When the first successful airplane flight took place in 1903 nothing seemed impossible for humans to accomplish. However, the outbreak of the First World War stopped the western world in its tracks. Over twenty million people died in the four-year war. Then in the last year of the war an influenza epidemic spread around the entire world, killing between twenty and forty million more people in two years. Such catastrophes as this can either drive people to seek God or cause them to blame God. Many did turn to God in the following years but even more turned away. Over much of the twentieth century society became secularised. That means that people rejected Christianity, saying that God either didn't care or didn't even exist. During previous centuries people who said that out loud were considered odd or dangerous. Now it was becoming an accepted way to think and talk.

However, God's plans were going ahead, whether people believed in him or not. He still had plans for preachers and teachers in the twentieth century. One of those preachers was born in Africa.

Festo Kivengere was born in south-western Uganda into the royal family of his tribe. Festo spent the first ten years of his life learning to care for the family's cows and living in a round grass hut. However, his life was changed when a 'pink lady' arrived in his village. The missionary, Constance Hornby, received her name because of her sunburned skin. At first she was treated with fear, until they came to understand what she was offering: a school for children. When Festo's grandfather, the king, heard about the school, he agreed to send their tribe's children. Festo traded in his calf-skin clothing for a western shirt and shorts, and his milking duties for textbooks and homework. Festo discovered he loved to learn and study so much that he hardly ever complained about the six-mile walk to school.

Festo was also interested in the Christian God and became convinced that he should serve God. However, as Festo grew up, he drifted away from Christianity and spent his time training to be a teacher. When he was twenty-one years old, a revival began in his area. So many people were converted that the government complained. The Christians were paying back the taxes they'd previously refused to pay and were returning things they had stolen. The queues were so long government clerks couldn't get their regular work done. At this time Festo was also converted. Now the school teacher was going to be God's preacher.

Festo continued to teach for many years. On School holidays he joined forces with other evangelists and they preached together in many African countries. Finally, after Festo had been married for quite a while and most of his girls were grown, he knew God was calling him to full-time ministry as an evangelist. He went to study at a seminary and he joined Billy Graham and others to preach around the world. But it was back home in Uganda where God had more work for Festo to do. When he was ordained a bishop in the Anglican Church of Uganda, his life took an unexpected and dangerous twist.

He Just Couldn't be Silent

Uganda 1973

◆◆◆◆◆ ■ ◆◆◆◆◆

Bishop Festo slowed his speed as he drove into the city of Kampala. As usual the traffic was everywhere: bicycles and boda-bodas weaving in and out of traffic and people dashing in between. The streets were full of noise and colourful umbrellas amidst the red dust that rose as each car drove by. The bright sunshine glinted off the windows of tall and short buildings. For a few minutes, fifty-four-year-old Festo imagined that all was well in the capital city of Uganda. But then the traffic began to part around a pile of bodies in the middle of the road. Festo hastily wound up his window as the breeze brought the stench of decay into his car. And he began to pray quietly for the families of those who had been so brutally murdered.

Still feeling shaken at the terrible spectacle, Festo arrived at the diocesan offices near the Anglican cathedral. He had come to meet with Archbishop Sabiti and his fellow bishops to discuss the plans and concerns each had for their diocese. As he entered the building, he was met by a deacon who motioned him into a room where the bishops were already gathered around a radio. They were listening to the voice of President Idi Amin with fearful expressions on their faces. What had their dictator leader done now?

As they listened, the president railed against all those whom he claimed had conspired against his government, and then he announced a list of the people that he had ordered arrested for treason. Each person was to be taken to their home region and shot in public as a lesson to all. Everyone in each district was commanded to attend the executions. Festo heard the names of three men he knew from his home district of Kigezi and his heart sank.

When the broadcast finished, everyone remained silent. This was not the first time public executions had been announced. The bishops thought of their parishioners and the comfort and hope they needed to preach to them, even as they felt the same fear and uncertainty that was now part of life in Uganda.

Suddenly Festo spoke. 'Where is your telephone?'

The deacon, who stood in the doorway, said, 'Out here,' and he led Festo to the heavy black instrument that sat on a table in the corridor.

Festo picked up the receiver and said to the operator, 'Please put me through to the President. I wish to speak to him.'

The deacon gasped, but Festo ignored him as a voice sounded on the other end of the line. Taking a deep breath, Festo began, 'I am Bishop Festo Kivengere of the Kigezi District. I would like to meet with President Idi Amin Dada today, if possible.' There was a pause as the man on the other end told him to wait. Then to Festo's amazement, the voice told him that the president would see him now. 'I will come right away,' Festo replied and replaced the receiver back in its cradle with a shaking hand.

He turned to find the bishops standing in the corridor with the deacon staring at him. Before any of them could speak, he calmly told them he would have to postpone meeting with them until after he had spoken with the president.

'We will pray for your safety,' Archbishop Sabiti said quietly. 'May God go with you.'

'Thank you. This is my duty. I cannot keep silent in the face of such persecution.'

Festo drove to the parliament buildings where the President kept his office. After identifying himself to the heavily armed guards at the gate, Festo was waved through and told to leave his car next to the large tank parked in the courtyard. He was met by more armed guards and swiftly taken inside the building and through a maze of corridors until they reached an office. After knocking, the guards thrust Festo inside and closed the door.

The office was elegantly furnished with an enormous oak desk, and a large padded chair, along with several expensive antique chairs and small tables set about the room. In one of those chairs sat a little boy. Festo smiled at him and nodded, but the boy's only response was to look over to the tall, broad-shouldered man who stood looking out of the window. Slowly the man turned and Festo saw the feared President in full military dress, complete with a chest of shiny medals. For a moment Festo forgot to breathe. Then the President's wide face broke into a wide grin.

'Welcome Bishop. You have a good word for me?' The imposing man stood with his arms crossed over his chest. In spite of the smile, he didn't look friendly.

Festo took a deep breath and prayed for God to give him the right words.

'Your Excellency, I am troubled about your announcement of the public executions of the men who have been arrested. You have often said that you hear God, and God created human life in his own image, and therefore I plead that these men be given a chance to defend themselves.' Pausing for breath, Festo looked at the little boy who was sitting very still. 'You see this little boy of yours, sir? God will give him as long as he needs to grow into a man. So that when you think of taking away life, first give it as long as possible before taking it away.'

At first President Amin said nothing. Then he nodded. 'Thank you, Bishop Festo, for your words. I will think about them.' Then he grabbed a riding crop on his desk and rapped it on the desk several times. The door swung open. Two guards quickly escorted Festo out of the parliament building and to his car. Festo didn't start breathing normally until he had driven at least a mile away. Thank you, God, for keeping me safe, he prayed.

Sadly, Festo's plea for the men did no good. Their execution was set for 19th February in Kabale. So Festo asked for and received permission to visit the men before they were shot. He wanted to make sure they heard the gospel and had a chance to repent of their sins before they died. But what he thought would be a quiet pastoral visit in the cells turned out to be anything but that.

The execution day arrived and all the people of Kigezi District had been ordered to gather in the huge sports stadium in Kabale. Then the three men in handcuffs and leg chains were marched into the centre by their firing squad. After them, Festo and two other ministers were escorted by two guards onto the stadium floor. The enormous crowd was silent, but when the condemned men saw Festo one called out.

'Bishop Festo! Thank you for coming,' he said with excitement. 'I wanted to tell you. The day I was arrested, in my prison cell, I asked the Lord Jesus to come into my heart. He came in and forgave me all my sins! Heaven is now open and there is nothing between me and my God! Please tell my wife and children that I am going to be with Jesus. Ask them to accept him into their lives as I did.'

Festo was stunned. He had come to comfort these men with the gospel and God had already spoken to them.

Another man called out, 'I, too, am saved. I had wandered from the Lord and became involved in political confusion. But since my arrest I have confessed my sins and he has forgiven me and now I have peace. Please tell my parents. They have been praying for me for a long time.'

Many heard their confessions of faith, but Festo could tell by the confusion on the soldiers' faces that they didn't understand the local dialect. So Festo translated what the prisoners had said. The soldiers were dumbfounded to see men who were about to be shot with smiles on their faces. They motioned for Festo and the others to step aside and the prisoners stood together in a group, waving to the crowd. The people waved back. Upset by this unusual behaviour, the soldiers didn't take time to blindfold the prisoners. They just raised their guns and fired and the three young men fell to the ground.

Festo returned home that day with his wife Mera. Both were still feeling the shock of the day's events, so they sat quietly on their porch, listening to the noise of the insects and birds in the trees.

'Will the killings ever stop?' Mera asked, knowing Festo had no answer. 'Everyone I speak with knows of someone who has been taken, tortured or killed. And so many ask why God allows this.'

'Look at what Jesus had to suffer on the cross for us and he was sinless,' Festo replied. 'We are full of sin and rebellion. Only Christ can bring the peace that we need in this country. He can even change the heart of our president.'

'Hummmpf,' Mera replied ungraciously. 'He's an evil man.'

Festo reached over and laid his hand on his wife's. 'We were all born in sin. We all have rebelled against God. Idi Amin has just been more open about what is in his heart. We must pray for him that God will save him. And someone must present the gospel to him.'

Mera turned to him with a fearful expression. 'It doesn't need to be you!'

Festo shrugged. 'Everyone needs to hear God's Word. If God gives me the opportunity, I will speak.'

During that year over 90,000 people were killed and Festo had several opportunities to meet with the president to reproach him for his cruelty to the Ugandan people. Each time God preserved Festo's life. President Idi Amin greeted Festo pleasantly, listened to what he said and then dismissed him with thanks. Festo's visits didn't stop the violence, but he didn't give up. Meanwhile he kept up his busy schedule of dividing his time between his diocese and his speaking engagements around Africa and Europe. Festo was also invited to participate in the Lausanne Conference on World Evangelism in Switzerland the following year. Over 2,700 minsters and evangelists from 150 countries met together to discuss world evangelism and what they could be doing. Festo rejoiced to meet so many who were committed to preaching God's Word to as many people around the world as possible.

However, when he returned home, Uganda was in even worse shape than when he left. The president had deported all the Asian people from the country and as a result the economy was failing. The Asian people had owned many businesses in Uganda and, when they took their shops and money away from the country there were fewer jobs and much less money. Now lack of food was added to people's fear of arrest and torture.

And so it went for the next three years; Festo continued to preach in various African countries in between taking care of the people and business in his diocese. Festo loved to preach and large crowds would gather to hear him tell the stories of the Bible, always bringing people to the cross where Jesus chose to die for the sins of the world. Festo knew that every person needed to hear that God was calling them to repentance.

The year 1977 began with joy for Festo and Mera. Their first grandchild was born in Kampala to their oldest daughter, Peace. On their way back from a preaching tour, Festo and Mera stopped in to see the newest member of their family. Then they returned home to Kabale in time for Festo to preach at an ordination service. Festo preached from the verses in Acts 20 where Paul tells the Ephesian church that their leaders must guard the church from teachers of heresy and use their authority to build up the church. But before he finished, Festo looked out over the congregation of 30,000 people who sat before him in the hot sun. Not only were Christians present, but so were Muslims, government officials and even security guards. God prompted him to add these words:

'How are you using your authority in the government? Do you help the people that God has placed in your charge, or do you crush their faces in the dust?'

People began to shift uncomfortably while they stole glances at the security guards. But Festo continued for several minutes condemning the brutality of the government and telling them that they would have to answer to God for their actions. Everyone breathed a sigh of relief when the service came to an end without violent reaction. But Festo's sermon was reported to the president.

A couple of weeks later a telegram from Kampala arrived from the new Archbishop Janina Luwum. The message related in a few sentences that the archbishop's house was raided the previous night. The guards were looking for illegal weapons that could be used against the government. They found nothing, of course, but they threatened to come back. They also raided Bishop Yona's home.

Festo suddenly felt very angry. He couldn't ignore this action, so he jumped in his car with Mera and headed for Kampala. Once there, he met with the other bishops who were also upset over the raids. The fifteen bishops spent the next few days discussing what to write in the letter to send to President Idi Amin. By the end of the discussion, the letter was a long one, condemning the government for its treatment of the church and the Ugandan people, for the violence, false accusations and the attempt to force many to convert to Islam. They concluded the letter by asking for an audience with him to discuss these matters further.

Five days later, Archbishop Janina was summoned to meet with the president alone. As the archbishop went to the meeting, the rest of the bishops gathered to pray for his safety. A few hours later, he returned with the report that Idi Amin was angry with them and he still believed that the archbishop was hiding weapons to help the rebels. So once more the bishops sat down to write another letter, this time in defence of their archbishop, but before the letter could be sent Archbishop Janina was summoned once more, this time to meet government officials, along with the president. And this time, six of the bishops, including Festo, went with him.

They drove in two cars up to the International Conference Centre. They were startled to see over 1,000 soldiers surrounding a large group of governors, administrators, diplomats and religious leaders on the spacious grounds of the Centre. At one end stood President Idi Amin along with the vice-president and many open suitcases of automatic weapons. The archbishop and bishops stood in their ceremonial robes in the hot sun before their accusers. Festo could see the hatred in their eyes.

As they stood there, the vice-president began reading out false accusations against Archbishop Janina, pointing to the displayed weapons as evidence of his treason. The archbishop shook his head in denial, but he was ignored. The vice-president rambled on with accusation after accusation.

'They are going to kill me,' Archbishop Janina whispered, 'but I am not afraid.'

Suddenly the vice-president called out, 'What should we do with such traitors?'

'Kill them! Kill them!' the soldiers shouted.

Festo's heart began to thud in his chest. Was this his last day on earth? Would the soldiers shoot them here? Or would they be arrested and tortured first? Please give us strength and courage, he prayed.

But just as suddenly the vice-president said, 'No, we will give them a fair trial. Soldiers, take them into the centre.'

Dazed from the heat and the shock, Festo and the others walked toward the building. No one spoke. Once inside they were put in a room and told to wait without talking. They all sat down on chairs and waited, each praying quietly. Two soldiers stood guard inside the room by the door with machine guns in their hands.

After what seemed a long time, a captain entered the room and dismissed them. 'You may go home now, except for the archbishop. He is to come with me for a private audience with the president.'

Festo was about to object when Archbishop Janina spoke. 'I can see the hand of the Lord in this,' he said with a smile, and then meekly followed the captain out of the room.

At the urging of the guards, the rest of the bishops left the building and headed for their cars. Festo and Bishop Wani waited in their car for two hours in hopes that the archbishop would be released. The others had returned to tell the church and the archbishop's family what had happened. But then the soldiers came over to the car and told them to go home. The archbishop had been arrested.

The next morning the radio announcer said the archbishop had been killed in a car accident, but Festo and the others knew it was a lie. Their archbishop had been murdered. Now the bishops knew they had to return to their own diocese to care for their people. Who knew who would be next to be arrested and shot?

As Festo and Mera packed up their car a message arrived for them. The young man just passed a folded piece of paper to them and ran away. Inside was a warning. Idi Amin had placed Festo at the top of his death list. Without wasting any more time, they jumped in the car and drove at high speed to Kabale.

Usually when Festo drove into his home city nestled in green valleys and hills he would relax, but not today. As they drove down the main streets they saw military police everywhere. Some were driving around in army vehicles and others were walking along the streets with guns drawn, looking inside homes and businesses as they passed by. People scuttled by them, heading for their homes as quickly as possible. When Festo drove by one of their neighbours, he flagged them down.

'The soldiers are at your house. You cannot go home. There are friends waiting for you near the church, but be careful.' Then the man ran away.

'What do we do?' Festo asked Mera. 'Should I follow Archbishop Janina's example and let them take me? Or do we run?'

'I don't know,' Mera replied. 'I know I want you to be safe, but I don't know what God wants you to do. So let's go to our friends and see what they say.'

Festo nodded and turned the car in the direction toward the church. Before they reached it, someone else recognised their car and motioned them into a property full of bushes.

'Leave your car here where it can't be seen from the road and come with me.'

Following the man into the house, Festo and Mera were met by a small group of Christians who hugged and kissed them. 'We thought you were dead. There were reports of your death on the radio. Praise God you are alive.'

After prayer and discussion they convinced Festo that he must flee rather than stay and be arrested. 'Remember how God rescued Peter from prison? He will find a way to rescue you, too. We couldn't deal with the death of two bishops in one week,' they all told him.

Since Festo's car was known to the authorities, a young couple offered to drive Festo and Mera across the border into Rwanda in their Land Rover vehicle. So with nothing but the clothes they had gone to Kampala with, they headed for the border. The road was treacherous, both because it wasn't well paved and because soldiers were everywhere looking for Festo. After several re-routings the Land Rover came to a stop just out of sight of the roadblock set up by the border crossing.

Looking up at the tall mountains, Festo asked Mera with a smile, 'Feel like mountain climbing?'

She sighed. 'I suppose we have no choice. It's the only way out. I wish I'd worn better shoes.'

So after thanking their drivers, the middle-aged couple began their trek over the mountains to safety.

The Fancy Hat Teacher

Henrietta Mears had been a Chemistry and Drama teacher in Minnesota, U.S.A. for a number of years when she was offered a job in California in 1928. First Presbyterian Church of Hollywood hired her to be their Director of Christian Education. Henrietta, known for her fancy hats, loved to teach children and teens. She had been converted as a young child and taught her first Sunday school at age twelve. So to be able to combine her love for God with her love for teaching was a wonderful opportunity.

First Presbyterian's Sunday school already had 450 children and teens when Henrietta began. However, she was shocked to discover that the curriculum lessons were full of incorrect doctrines, teaching such things as the miracles in the Bible were not true. So Henrietta packaged it back up and returned it to the publisher. But what should she give the Sunday school teachers for their classes? So Henrietta decided to write her own curriculum that taught the truths found in the Bible. She was wielding the Sword of Truth with her pen and paper.

Over the next few years the Sunday school grew from 450 to 4,000. Other churches heard about the exciting things happening at First Presbyterian and asked Henrietta for copies of her curriculum. At first it was easy. She and her secretary made extra copies and sent them out. But as the requests became too numerous for Henrietta to manage, she decided to start a publishing company called *Gospel Light*.

Over the years Henrietta's classes and curriculum influenced a lot of men and women. Through her, they learned God's Truth and went on to serve God in various ways; people like the evangelist Billy Graham and Bill Bright, the founder of Campus Crusade.

Wielding the Sword

Festo and Mera made it safely into Rwanda where they stayed with friends for a few days. From there they moved to California in the United States to a home provided for them by some generous friends. Festo was exiled from Uganda for two years, but he kept in touch with his church and his daughters through letters. He also spoke out about what Idi Amin was doing in Uganda. Most of the world had been unaware of the suffering of the Ugandan people because the country had been closed to the news media. Meanwhile, Festo carried on preaching the gospel.

In 1979 President Idi Amin was defeated in a war with Tanzania and he fled to Libya. Uganda was now freed from their cruel president and Festo was able to return home. He wanted to help rebuild his country, preach the Good News to those who had not heard it and encourage those believers who had suffered so much. Most of all he wanted to teach the people about forgiveness and reconciliation. Festo Kivengere died in 1989.

Festo wasn't the only preacher in the last century. In fact the twentieth century was blessed with many excellent preachers and teachers. The work they began has carried over into our century.

Billy Graham

Billy Graham is probably the best known evangelist of the twentieth century. He was born in 1918 on a dairy farm in the state of North Carolina in the United States. Until he was sixteen he had very little idea what he would do after he finished school. But that year he attended a revival meeting and was converted. He also began to feel a call to become a preacher. He joined the Baptist church and went to Florida Bible Institute and Wheaton College for training. He graduated in 1943, married Ruth Bell and became pastor of Western Spring Baptist Church near Chicago. And that could have been the beginning of his ministry in various churches but God had something else in mind for Billy, something that would use his particular talents to present the Gospel to a great many people.

Torrey Johnson, a preacher, had two radio programmes with hymns and preaching and he asked Billy to take over one of them. Billy was thrilled to do so, but worried about who would tune in to hear an unknown pastor. So he asked George Beverly Shea, a well-known singer, to help him. Bev. Shea sang hymns and Billy preached. The programme was heard in several states of the Midwest and it caught on. Billy had an exciting way of presenting God's truth and people wanted to hear more. The following year Billy was asked to become a full-time evangelist for Youth for Christ International. For the next several years he travelled all over North America and Europe preaching to young people. Many were converted. Billy then decided to expand his ministry to include people of all ages and in 1949 held his first crusade in Los Angeles. As Billy's fame grew, so did the attendance at his crusades in many North American cities as well as countries around the world. Billy also saw the value of using modern inventions for God. He started a new radio programme called *Hour of Decision*, founded a movie production company called *World Wide Pictures* and began a magazine called *Decision*. He also wrote a number of books. All these things were used to tell people about the gospel.

At the time of this writing, Billy Graham is ninety-four years old, and the work he began is being carried on by his son Franklin and many others.

Dr Martyn Lloyd-Jones

Martyn Lloyd-Jones had no plans to be a preacher when he was growing up. He spent the first fifteen years of his life in Wales, living with his family and studying hard at school. He had decided to become a doctor. When his father's business failed, the family moved to London to start in a new business. In keeping with his plans, Martyn attended grammar school and then became a medical student at St Bartholomew's Hospital. He did so well in his training that he was eventually hired as Dr Horder's assistant. Dr Horder was the Royal Physician, treating King George V and his family.

Martyn was brought up in a Christian home. He went to church, read his Bible and prayed. Everyone, including Martyn, thought he was a Christian. But about the time Martyn was twenty-one, God began to work in his heart. Martyn came to realise he was a sinful person and he needed to repent and ask God's forgiveness. At Easter in 1925 Martyn was converted, and he was grateful for the joy and peace God's love gave him. Along with his conversion came a call to be a preacher. So he quit his position with the Royal Physician, married his sweetheart Bethan Phillips, and moved back to Wales to minister to a church in Aberavon, Port Talbot.

Because he had been mistaken all those years about being a Christian, Martyn focused his preaching on the importance of salvation by faith in Jesus Christ. Through his powerful preaching, many people in his church were converted over the next eleven years. He also provided them with medical care whenever they were in need. In 1938 Martyn became assistant minister to Westminster Chapel in London. Five years later he became sole minister and remained there for twenty-five years. Besides his Sunday preaching, Martyn also taught a series on the book of Romans on Friday evenings. It was so well done that the series was published in a fourteen volume set for other preachers and teachers to use.

John Murray

Not all those who have served God in the twentieth century were as famous as Billy Graham or Martyn Lloyd-Jones. Some were just quietly faithful to God and carried out their tasks of preaching and teaching in a steady way. One of them was John Murray. John was born in a small village in the Scottish Highlands in 1898. When John was just a boy, his teachers noticed how very clever he was and they encouraged him to go on with his studies. However, in 1917, when he was nineteen, he was conscripted into the Black Watch regiment and sent to France to fight in World War I. He was wounded in one eye and had to have it removed. It was replaced with a glass eye, which looked real enough, but because of his injury he was sent home instead of returning to the war zone.

Even though his sight was impaired, John went on to university; first in Glasgow and then to Princeton in the USA and then back to Scotland to study at New College in Edinburgh. Also during that time he travelled about Scotland, USA and Canada, preaching in Presbyterian churches and making many friends. In 1929 he was invited to return to Princeton to teach systematic theology to young men studying for the ministry.

John was very excited about the opportunity but was upset to find when he arrived that Princeton Seminary was in a mess. There was a big fight between the professors. On one side were those who said the Bible was infallible, Jesus is God not just a man, and that he died for our sins and came back to life again. On the other side were professors who said the Bible was a good book but not the only one, they doubted that Jesus was really God's Son, and therefore couldn't say that Jesus was able to die for our sins and he probably didn't come back to life. John knew that second group of professors were wrong, so after one year of teaching he left Princeton along with four other professors and together they founded Westminster Theological Seminary in Philadelphia in 1930.

John taught students for the next thirty-seven years. His lessons were not full of funny stories nor did he use anything but his voice to teach, but his students did receive excellent, systematic explanations of the Christian faith that they used when they became pastors, missionaries or served God in their secular jobs. He instructed a generation in the truths of God with both his teaching and his writings. He also continued to travel and preach, especially in Canada, where he found a 'church home' in a small Presbyterian Church in Chesley, Ontario that he loved. Many from that congregation remember John Murray as a quiet, godly man, whose pulpit prayers stirred their hearts. John retired to Scotland in 1966, where he married Valerie Knowlton. They had two children before John died of cancer in 1975.

John Stott

John Stott was born in London in 1921. His father was a doctor and the family was comfortably well off. John was sent to the best schools, and with his flair for learning new languages, his parents hoped he would become a diplomat. However, in 1938 John was converted and felt a call to serve God as a minister. His father, in particular, was very disappointed in his son, but John chose to go into the ministry anyway.

In 1945 John was ordained a deacon in All Souls Anglican Church in London. Five years later he became the Rector [minister] and remained so for most of his life. John had both a gift for preaching and for writing. He began editing, and sometimes writing, a series called *The Bible Speaks Today* that eventually contained a commentary on each book of the Bible. These commentaries were meant to be read by everyone, not just theology students, and have been very helpful to people over the years. John also wrote many other books that have been used to bring many to Christ.

John became involved with international ministries first through Billy Graham. When Billy Graham came to England to preach, John was one of the people who assisted him. Soon John was travelling all over the world visiting every continent and preaching in many churches. John knew the importance of preaching the gospel and of working with other preachers and teachers to make sure as many people heard about God's Good

News as possible. When John wasn't travelling he also acted as one of Queen Elizabeth II's chaplains.

In 1966 John met with Martyn Lloyd-Jones and they had a disagreement. Martyn was distressed that some Anglican minsters were questioning the Bible and what it taught. His solution was to tell Christians to leave the Anglican Church and not associate with ministers who didn't teach the gospel. But John said, no. Instead he thought the Christians should stay in the Anglican Church and preach to those who didn't believe, so they would know the truth. The disagreement caused a lot of problems because people began to take sides. Twelve years later they made up their quarrel, agreeing that each should serve God as God led them.

John continued his preaching until age seventy-six when he retired. He wrote one more book, *The Radical Disciple,* before he died in 2011.

Elisabeth Elliot

Elisabeth Elliot was born in 1926 in Belgium where her parents were missionaries. When Elisabeth was very young her parents moved to the Philadelphia area in the USA. Her father became the editor of a magazine called *The Sunday School Times.* As Elisabeth grew up she felt called to be a missionary, so she went to Wheaton College for training. There she learned ancient languages and how to begin writing down languages that had never been written before.

In 1953 she went to Ecuador to work with the Quichua Indians. Jim Eliot, who Elisabeth had met at Wheaton, also went to Ecuador planning to contact Indian tribes that had remained hidden in the rain forest. Elisabeth and Jim were married that year and had a baby girl named Valerie two years later. In 1956 Jim and four other male missionaries decided to contact the Auca people, a fierce group of warriors who hadn't allowed any white people into their area before. At first the meeting appeared to go well, but then the tribesmen turned on the missionaries and killed them all. Elisabeth was now a young widow with a one-year-old child. Instead of returning to the USA, Elisabeth wrote a book about what had happened to her husband called *Through Gates of Splendour*. Through a remarkable providence of God, Elisabeth was then able to go and live with the very tribe who had killed her husband, along with her daughter and one other female missionary. Her willingness to forgive and love those people brought many of them to Christ.

In 1963 Elisabeth and Valerie returned to live in the USA. Elisabeth continued to write books. She wrote about her husband's life and published his journals which have inspired many to become missionaries. She also wrote about living the Christian life, dealing with suffering and loneliness, and about lessons she had learned from God. In all, Elisabeth has written twenty books which have helped many people. She has also been a speaker at women's conferences, a teacher at Gordon Conwell College and presented a weekly radio programme called 'Gateway to Joy'. She married again in 1969 but her husband died of cancer four years later. She married for the third time in 1977 and now lives in retirement with her husband in Massachusetts.

Why Does It Matter?

There is a saying that goes 'the more things change the more they stay the same.' Sounds impossible, doesn't it? But let's think about it. Lots of things have changed over the centuries. Carrying mobile phones, sending space ships to investigate Mars or even microwaving a dinner would not be understood by people in medieval times. Any more than we would understand about eating without forks, being bled with leeches when we are ill, or having no 'rights' before a king or lord of the manor. But even though these things have changed, the basic needs of the church and the world have not changed. Twenty-first century people still need to hear the gospel, just as they did in the Roman Empire. Christians still need to be taught correct doctrine and encouraged in their daily lives. God is still using preachers and teachers to sound his message.

Remember when we looked at false teachers at the beginning of this book? The heresies they taught then are still here today. The Jehovah's Witnesses believe that Jesus was only a human teacher and not the Son of God, just as the Arians taught centuries ago. Scientology, a religion invented in the twentieth century, teaches that people need a special type of knowledge to reach sinless perfection. And they also teach that our spirits are kept captive by our bodies and need to be freed. Sounds like the Gnostic heresy, doesn't it?

The religion of the Roman Empire was based on worshipping many pagan gods, working hard to keep them all happy with various sacrifices, rituals and vows. There are still people today who work hard to live 'good' lives in order to earn their salvation. Muslims have set prayer patterns, ways of dressing, and many rules to follow in order to please Allah and be rewarded with heaven. This sounds a bit like the Manichaeism that Augustine was caught up in before his conversion. Throughout history, groups of people have worshipped trees, mountains, the sun and other parts of nature. Even today in our 'advanced' culture some people worship 'mother earth' or study the auras of living things to discern their health.

Then there is atheism, which is popular in our twenty-first century culture. Atheists say there is no God. He is only someone dreamed up to make weak people feel better. They say only humans matter in their lifetime and there is no meaning to life. We are just born into the world, live our lives and then die. Atheists can live as they please, whether doing good or bad, because they believe it doesn't matter.

The world still needs God's bubbling fountains, his preachers and teachers, to keep spreading the gospel to each new generation who need to hear God's truth. And each new generation of Christians must be taught to guard against wrong teaching by hearing God's Word preached correctly and studying the Scriptures. Paul warns about this in his letter to the Ephesian church. He uses the picture of putting on armour to protect the Christian from heresies and the attacks of the evil one.

> In all circumstances take up the shield of faith, with which you can
> extinguish all the flaming darts of the evil one; and take the helmet
> of salvation, and the sword of the Spirit, which is the word of God,
> praying at all times in the Spirit, with all prayer and supplication.[1]

Preachers and teachers must use God's Word as a sword, wielding it in their preaching and teaching so that all might know The Truth.

So why does this matter to us? We aren't preachers or teachers, at least, not yet. However, even at your age when you hear God's truth proclaimed you must respond. You must worship God, serve him and share the good news of the gospel with others. You, too, can wield The Sword of Truth.

---

[1] Ephesians 6:16-18a

STRANGE WORDS AND PHRASES

A.D.: short form for the Latin phrase Anno Domini, 'In the Year of our Lord'. Now the numbers start to go forward instead of backward as the B.C. dates did.

Alienation: to withdraw or separate.

Atrium: a large central room open to the sky.

B.C.: Before Christ was born on earth. B.C. dates are recorded backwards, like a countdown to when Jesus was born on earth.

Boda-bodas: Ugandan word for motorcycles.

Book of Homilies: Two books of sermons published in sixteenth century England to be used to educate priests and bishops at the beginning of the Reformation about how to preach and about what was changing in the church.

Bread spoon: a thick piece of bread, roughly shaped into a scoop to assist in eating. The bonus was the 'spoon' could be eaten at the end of the meal.

Castellan: a governor of a castle.

Cell: small bedroom in a monastery or friary.

Cession: to stop.

Chapel: a place of worship, smaller in size than a church.

Codex: an ancient manuscript in book form.

Comforter: a type of duvet.

Concubine: a woman living with a man as his wife, but not married to him.

Consul: a chief magistrate in the Roman Empire.

Deacon: in the early medieval church, the office of Deacon was an administrative one. The deacon not only handled the church's money, distributing it where it was needed, but he also assisted his bishop, acting as a secretary.

Deport: to send out of a country, usually not allowed to return.

Dialect: a regional variety of a language, with differences in pronunciation, grammar or vocabulary.

Diocese: in the Anglican Church, a bishop is appointed to a particular geographical area called a diocese. His job is to pastor the pastors of the churches in that area as well as deal with the business of the church (building schools, seminary education, financial matters, etc.).

Doctrine: something that is taught.

Duchies: the territories ruled by a duke or duchess.

Endowment: a fund donated by individuals to an institution that is invested and becomes a source of income for the institution.

Eucharist: the Lord's Supper.

Fasting: going without food in order to pray and sing the psalms.

Fraudulently: using trickery or deceit.

Fresco: a painting on fresh, moist plaster using water colours. The painting dries and becomes part of the wall.

Friar: a member of a religious order that combines monastic life with religious life, mainly preaching, in the community.

Friary: a monastery of friars.

Genevan gown: a long black robe often worn by clergy.

Gout: a form of acute arthritis that causes severe pain and swelling in the joints. It most commonly affects the big toe, but may also affect the heel, ankle, hand, wrist, or elbow.

Guarantor: someone who promises to pay a sum of money.

Habit: long sleeved, long tunic, with a separate hood worn by monks.

Heretic: a person who holds a belief, opinion or doctrine contrary to the teachings of Christianity.

Impromptu: not prepared ahead of time.

Inaugural lecture: It was and still is customary for professors who are promoted to a new position to give a public lecture on their subject of expertise.

Indulgences: paying money to cancel out a sin. The papacy used the money to fund building projects.

Inquisitor: someone who makes inquiries, often in a harsh or severe manner.

Institutes: can mean to organise something, especially for educating people about an idea. This is the reason Calvin used this word in the title of his famous book *The Institutes of the Christian Religion*.

Lenten season (Lent): forty days before Easter, a time when Christians spend more time in prayer and fasting.

Liturgy: a prescribed form or set of forms for public worship.

Manse: a house set aside for the minister and his family to live in.

Mass: a worship service in the Roman Catholic Church, which contains prayers, praise, Scripture reading and a short sermon. It ends with the celebration of the Lord's Supper in which they believe that the bread and wine are miraculously turned into the actual body and blood of Christ.

Masters of the College: teachers or professors who had earned their Master's degree and received a license to teach at the university.

Mulled wine: wine heated with sugar and spices.

Orator: a public speaker.

Panegyric: a formal public speech that is given in praise of a person or thing.

Papal Bull: an official letter from the pope.

Pascha: a Greek word that refers to Easter, or the feast of the Resurrection of the Lord. The word means Passover, which is the meal Jesus ate with his disciples before his crucifixion and resurrection. People in the eastern part of the Christian church still use this word today for Easter.

Patriarch: the head of the Eastern Church in Constantinople.

Patron: a wealthy or influential supporter of an artist or literary person.

Pecuniary: having to do with money.

Penitent: someone who expresses sorrow for their sin.

Periwig: a wig worn by men in the 17th and 18th centuries.

Piazza: an Italian city square where people gather.

Placards: a poster or sign for public display.

Podesta: chief magistrate in a medieval Italian town or city.

Pope: means 'papa' or 'father' in Latin. It became the title of the Bishop of Rome around the sixth century.

Preaching tabs: two oblong pieces of white cloth tied around the neck. These were worn by clergy.

Praetorium: the official residence of the Roman governor.

Precentor: a clergyman who leads or directs a church choir.

Prefect: chief magistrate or governor.

Prefect of Rome: an official appointed by the emperor to rule the city of Rome in the empire. The word prefect means 'to stand in front of others'.

Preface: introductory remarks at the beginning of a book.

Proconsul: a governor or military commander.

Prime: a prayer service held at 6 a.m. each morning in a monastery or friary.

Recant: to withdraw a statement in a formal or public way.

Rector: a priest in charge of a church.

Rector of a university: head of a medieval university, usually a professor who was also a priest

Refectory: a dining hall in a monastery or friary.

Remorse: to deeply regret a wrong that has been committed.

Renunciation: to change your mind about something you agreed to do or believe.

Rhetoric: the art or study of using language (written or spoken) effectively and persuasively.

Rumford oven: a smaller chamber built into the side of an open fireplace, used for baking.

Sawyer: a person who saws timber for a living.

Seminary: a school of higher learning, not just religious studies. In the eighteenth century it usually meant a school for women because colleges were only open to men at that time.

Sloop: a fore and aft rigged sailboat with one mast.

Sorbonne: the theological college that is part of the University of Paris. The faculty or professors were powerful churchmen during medieval times.

Synod: a council or assembly of church officials

Systematic Theology: an orderly way of studying the Christian doctrines found in the Bible.

Tabernacle: Before Solomon built the temple in Jerusalem, the Israelites worshipped in a 'tent church' designed by God himself. See Exodus 26 for a description.

Toga: A loose flowing outer garment worn by the citizens of ancient Rome, made of a single piece of cloth.

Wield: to use effectively or expertly.

How many books/ DVDs does it take to write one book?

Anderson, Clive. *Travel with C.H. Spurgeon: In the footsteps of the 'Prince of Preachers'*. Epsom, Surrey: Day One Publications, 2002.

Augustine. *Confessions*. Translated and introduced by R.S. Pine-Coffin. Harmondsworth, Eng.: Penguin Books, 1961.

Baldwin, Joyce G. *1 & 2 Samuel: An introduction and commentary*. (Tyndale Old Testament Commentaries) Leicester, Eng.: Inter Varsity Press, 1988.

Barton, F. Whitfield. *Calvin and the Duchess*. Louisville, KY: John Knox Press, 1989.

Benjamin Franklin on Rev George Whitefield, 1739. National Humanities Center. http://nationalhumanitiescenter.org/pds/becomingamer/ideas/text2/franklinwhitefield.pdf (accessed March 2013).

Blackburn, Earl M. *John Chrysostom*. Carlisle, PA: EP Books, 2012.

Bruce, F.F. *The Book of the Acts* (The New International Commentary on the New Testament) Eerdmans, 1979.

Budgen, Victor. *On Fire for God: The Story of John Hus*. Welwyn, Hertfordshire, Eng.: Evangelical Press, 1983.

C. H. Spurgeon: the People's Preacher. Vision Video, 2010.

Calvin, John. *Institutes of the Christian Religion*. Philadelphia: Westminster Press, 1960.

Carr, Simonetta. *Augustine of Hippo*. Grand Rapids: Reformation Heritage Books, 2009.

Carr, Simonetta. *John Calvin*. Grand Rapids: Reformation Heritage Books, 2008

Chadwick, Henry. *Augustine of Hippo: A Life*. Oxford: Oxford University Press, 2009.

Chadwick, Henry. *The Early Church: Pelican History of the Church, 1*. Harmondsworth, Eng.: Penguin Books, 1967.

Chadwick, Owen. *The Reformation: The Pelican History of the Church, 3*. Harmondsworth, Eng.: Penguin Books, 1972.

Clasen, Sophronius. *St Anthony, Doctor of the Church* (translated by Ignatius Brady). Chicago: Franciscan Herald Press, 1973.

Coomes, Anne. *Festo Kivengere: A biography*. Eastbourne, Eng.: Monarch Publications, 1990.

Drive Thru History: Asia Minor with Dave Stotts. [DVD] Palmer Lake, CO: Coldwater Media, 2006.

ESV Study Bible. Crossway Bibles, 2008.

The 1400s edited by Stuart A. Kallen. (Headlines in History) San Diego, CA: Greenhaven Press, 2001.

Fradin, Dennis Brindell. *The Georgia Colony*. Chicago: Children's Press, 1989.

Frassetto, Michael. *The Great Medieval Heretics: Five Centuries of Religious Dissent*. New York: Blue Bridge, 2008.

Fudge, Thomas A. *Jan Hus: Religious Reform and Social Revolution in Bohemia*. London: I.B. Tauris, 2010.

Green, Elizabeth Alden. *Mary Lyon and Mount Holyoke: Opening the Gates*. Hanover, NH: University Press of New England, 1979.

Grun, Bernard. *The Timetables of History: A Horizontal Linkage of People and Events*. 4th ed. New York: Simon and Schuster, 2005.

Hinwood, Bonaventure. 'Word and Sacrament in St Anthony,' in *Antonianum: periodicum trimester*, v.53, no.3 (1978), pp. 471-492.

John Hus. Worchester, Pa: Gateway Films, 1980.

Kelly, J.N.D. *Golden Mouth: The story of John Chrysostom—Ascetic, Preacher, Bishop*. New York: Cornell University Press, 1995.

Laurence, Ray. *The Roman Empire: Rome and its Environs*. New York: Metro Books, 2008.

Markus, R.A. *Gregory the Great and his World*. Cambridge, UK: Cambridge University Press, 1997.

Marston, Elsa. *The Byzantine Empire*. Tarrytown, NY: Benchmark Books, 2003.

Norwich, John Julius. *Absolute Monarchs: A History of the Papacy*. New York: Random House, 2011.

Old, Hugh Oliphant. *The Reading and Preaching of the Scriptures in the Worship of the Christian Church*, v.1-7 Grand Rapids, Eerdmans, 1998-2010

Painting, Norman and Michael Day. *St Anthony: the Man who Found Himself*. Chicago: Franciscan Herald Press, 1957.

Parker, T. H. L. *Portrait of Calvin*. Philadelphia: Westminster Press, 1954.

Payne, Robert. *The Holy Fire: The story of the Fathers of the Eastern Church*. New York: Harper and Brothers, 1957.

Pollock, John. *George Whitefield and the Great Awakening*. Garden City, NY: Doubleday, 1972.

Retief, Frank. *Festo Kivengere*. (Bitesize Biographies) Faverdale North, Darlington, Eng.: EP Books, 2012.

Reymond, Robert L. *John Calvin: His Life and Influence*. Fearn, Tain, Ross-shire: Christian Focus Publications, 2004.

Richards, Jeffrey. *Consul of God: The life and times of Gregory the Great*. London: Routledge & Kegan Paul, 1980.

Steer, Roger. *Basic Christian: The inside story of John Stott*. Downers Grove, IL: Inter Varsity Press, 2009.

Stott, John. *The Spirit of the Church and the World: The message of Acts*. Downers Grove, IL: InterVarsity Press, 1990.

Thiede, Carsten P. *Simon Peter: from Galilee to Rome*. Grand Rapids: Zondervan, 1988.

Whitcomb, John C. *Chart of Old Testament Kings and Prophets*, 5th ed. Winona Lake, Ind.: Grace Theological Seminary, 1977.

Wills, Garry. *Saint Augustine*. New York: Penguin, 1999.

Wiseman, Donald J. *1 & 2 Kings: An Introduction and Commentary*. (Tyndale Old Testament commentaries) Downers Grove, IL: InterVarsity Press, 1993.

Withrow, Mindy and Brandon. *Perils and Peace: Chronicles of the Ancient Church*. Fearn, Tain, Ross-shire: Christian Focus Publicatons, 2005.

Young, M. *The Life and Times of Aonio Paleario, or a History of the Italian Reformers in the Sixteenth Century*. London: Bell and Daldy, 1860.

MAPS

EUROPE IN THE 14-16th CENTURIES

NORTH SEA

London

ENGLISH CHANNEL

Paris

Strasbo

Orleans

Bourges

Poitiers

Saintonge

FRANCE

NAVARRE

PORTUGAL

SPAIN

BRITAIN

Milan .

Rome

Ostia

Hippo
(Annaba)

Carthage
(Tunis)

ALGERIA

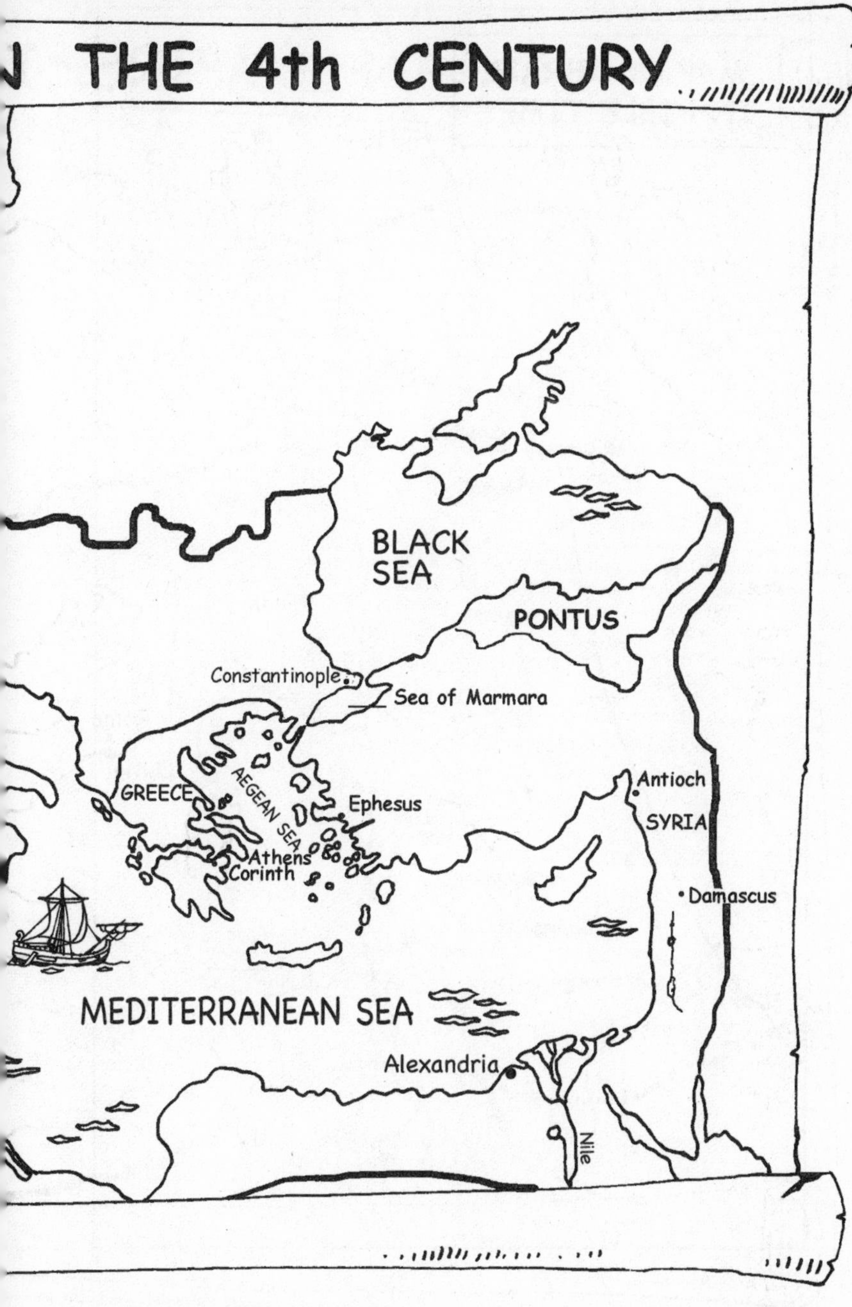

BLACK
SEA

PONTUS

Constantinople

Sea of Marmara

GREECE

AEGEAN SEA

Ephesus

Antioch

SYRIA

Athens
Corinth

Damascus

MEDITERRANEAN SEA

Alexandria

Nile

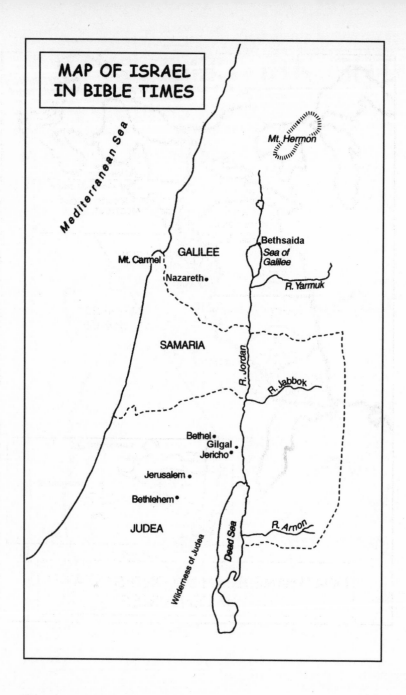

MAP OF ISRAEL
IN BIBLE TIMES

Mediterranean Sea

Mt. Hermon

Bethsaida
Sea of
Galilee

GALILEE

Mt. Carmel

Nazareth

R. Yarmuk

SAMARIA

R. Jordan

R. Jabbok

Bethel
Gilgal
Jericho

Jerusalem

Bethlehem

JUDEA

Wilderness of Judea

Dead Sea

R. Arnon

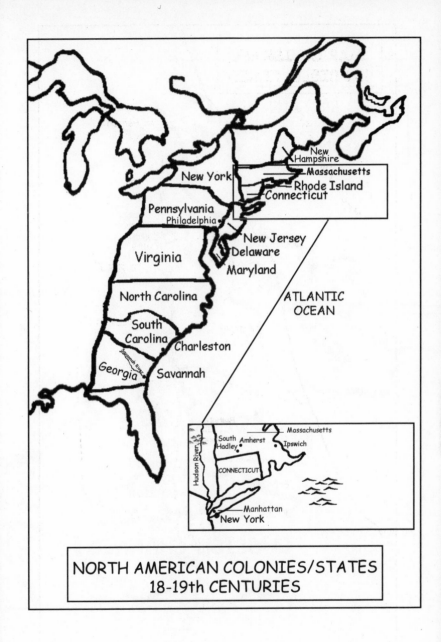

NORTH AMERICAN COLONIES/STATES
18-19th CENTURIES

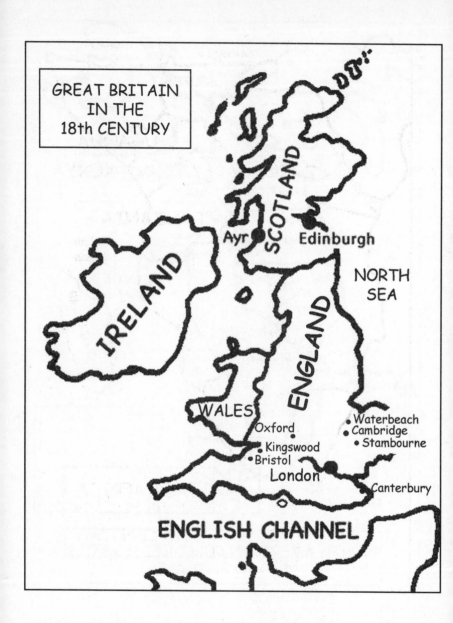

GREAT BRITAIN
IN THE
18th CENTURY

SCOTLAND

IRELAND

ENGLAND

WALES

NORTH
SEA

Ayr

Edinburgh

Waterbeach
Cambridge
Stambourne

Oxford

Kingswood
Bristol

London

Canterbury

ENGLISH CHANNEL

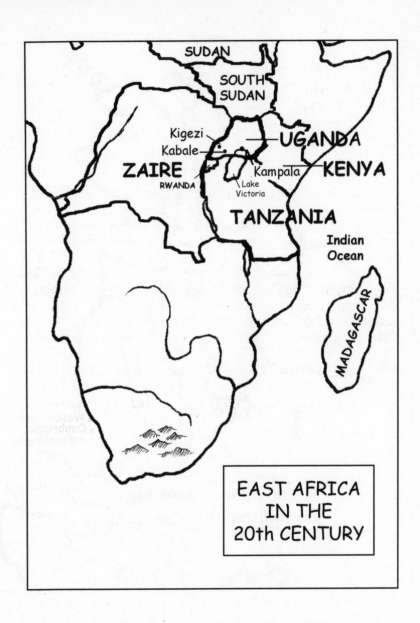

EAST AFRICA
IN THE
20th CENTURY

CHRISTIAN FOCUS PUBLICATIONS

Christian Christian CF4K Mentor
Focus Heritage

Christian Focus Publications publishes books for adults and children under its four main imprints: Christian Focus, CF4K, Mentor and Christian Heritage. Our books reflect our conviction that God's Word is reliable and Jesus is the way to know him, and live for ever with him.

Our children's publication list includes a Sunday School curriculum that covers pre-school to early teens, and puzzle and activity books. We also publish personal and family devotional titles, biographies and inspirational stories that children will love.

If you are looking for quality Bible teaching for children then we have an excellent range of Bible stories and age-specific theological books.

From pre-school board books to teenage apologetics, we have it covered!

Find us at our web page:
www.christianfocus.com

CF4 •K
Because you're never
too young to know Jesus